More praise for *The Truth About Leadership*

"I love *The Truth About Leadership*. Jim Kouzes and Barry Posner spell out ten fundamental truths about leadership and every one of them is right on. If you want to do a fact check on your leadership expertise, read this book!"

—*Ken Blanchard, co-author,* The One Minute Manager® *and* Leading at a Higher Level

"*The Truth About Leadership* is a rare and wonderful book that will become an essential guidebook for leaders in every sector at every level, at any point on their journey to leadership. Thank you, Jim and Barry, for sharing The Truth with us. There is no greater gift."

—*Frances Hesselbein, president and CEO,* Leader to Leader Institute

"Kouzes and Posner take a truly bold step in their new book about leadership fundamentals. Its impact comes from its relentless focus on what transcends time and endures globally in the arena of leadership, and in the compelling stories and illustrations that remind us all of what matters most."

—*Jon R. Katzenbach, co-author,* Leading Outside the Lines *and* The Wisdom of Teams

"This book is exactly what it purports to be: the 'truth' about leadership. It is exactly the right length, it covers everything it should, and leaves nothing out. Having read scores of books on the subject, I can comfortably say, it is the best one out there."

—Ken Wilcox, president and CEO,
SVB Financial Group

"In our work in government and leadership development, Kouzes and Posner's *The Leadership Challenge* has been our primary leadership guide. As our daughters begin to immerse themselves in Americorps and the world of work, we're sharing *The Truth About Leadership* with them. We're confident that these readable stories of everyday leaders and time-tested and research-tested principles will practically and intellectually arm them to change the world."

—Jennifer Granholm, Governor, State of
Michigan, and Dan Mulhern, First
Gentleman, State of Michigan, and
author of Everyday Leadership

"If Kouzes and Posner have any say in it, disjointed, prize-oriented, and loveless leaders will become a thing of the past. They provide us with a recipe for successful leadership by asking all of us to lead with passion, be an example, and make sure we're passionate about what we do."

—John Hope Bryant, author, Love Leadership *and*
founder, chairman, and CEO, Operation HOPE

"Reading this book made me feel as if I was in a conversation that I did not want to end. While there are many solid books about leadership, *The Truth About Leadership* is now the first book I will give others on their leadership journey."

—Teresa Roche, vice president and CLO, Agilent Technologies

"The glory of Kouzes and Posner's new book, *The Truth About Leadership*, isn't just in the ideas—you expect this kind of wisdom from the two most influential writers on leadership in our time—but in the voices and the data. You hear from everyday folks, not just the famous, about what it's like to be a successful leader in real-life settings. As for the numbers, has there ever been a leadership book so firmly grounded in empirical data drawn from literally millions of leaders?"

—Michael S. Malone, editor-in-chief of Edgelings.com *and author,* The Future Arrived Yesterday

"Leadership matters ... still. Another classic by Posner and Kouzes on the one topic that has impacted everyone, told in a very compelling and meaningful way. They have identified the most important characteristics of leadership that have withstood the test of time and captured them in this easy-to-read and captivating book."

—Sonia Clark, leader of Talent Strategy, Juniper Network

"Jim and Barry have written another masterful book to help us mere mortals on the never-ending journey of understanding what it takes to be a leader. I love this book because of its pragmatic approach, and because it seems to explain so simply the stuff that we intuitively know but somehow don't always keep at the front of our mind."

—*Greg Bourke, director, Human Resources, Vodafone Hutchison Australia*

"*The Truth About Leadership* should be a must-read for leaders and aspiring leaders. It offers timeless advice and insight, and real-world examples that anyone can relate to."

—*Charles Mak, Morgan Stanley's head of Private Wealth Management for Asia*

THE TRUTH

ABOUT

LEADERSHIP

The **NO-FADS,** HEART-OF-THE-MATTER **FACTS YOU NEED TO KNOW**

JAMES M. KOUZES
BARRY Z. POSNER

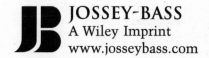

JOSSEY-BASS
A Wiley Imprint
www.josseybass.com

Published by Jossey-Bass
A Wiley Imprint
989 Market Street, San Francisco, CA 94103-1741—www.josseybass.com

Jossey-Bass books and products are available through most bookstores. To contact
Jossey-Bass directly call our Customer Care Department within the U.S. at 800-956-
7739, outside the U.S. at 317-572-3986, or fax 317-572-4002.

Jossey-Bass also publishes its books in a variety of electronic formats. Some content that appears in print may not be available in electronic books.

Library of Congress Cataloging-in-Publication Data

Kouzes, James M., 1945-
  The truth about leadership : the no-fads, heart-of-the-matter facts you need
to know / James M. Kouzes, Barry Z. Posner.
    p. cm.
  Includes index.
  ISBN 978-0-470-63354-0 (hardback)
  1. Leadership. 2. Executive ability. I. Posner, Barry Z. II. Title.
  HD57.7.K684 2010
  658.4'092—dc22

                             2010018715

Printed in the United States of America
FIRST EDITION

HB Printing   10 9 8 7 6 5 4 3 2 1

For Amanda and Nick.
Our own next-generation leaders.

CONTENTS

WHAT EVERYONE WANTS TO KNOW ABOUT LEADERSHIP

We've been traveling the world for three decades now, constantly researching the practices of exemplary leadership and the qualities people look for and admire in the leaders they would willingly follow. During and after our seminars and presentations, people ask us a lot of different questions, but there's always one thing that they all want to know: "What's new?"

No matter the age of the audience, the type of organizations they come from, or their nationalities, everyone wants to know what's changed since we first started studying leadership. They want to know how things are different now compared to how they were five, ten, twenty, or thirty years ago. So we tell them.

We tell them how *the context* of leadership has changed dramatically since we first asked people in the early 1980s to tell us about their personal best leadership experiences and about their most admired leaders. For example, we talk about how global terrorism has heightened uncertainty as political landscapes have changed. How global warming and scarcity of natural resources have made regions of the world unstable and created the need for more sustainable products and lifestyles. How the global economy has increased marketplace competition in the neighborhood and around the world and how financial institutions have exploded, imploded, and risen like phoenixes from the ashes. How the always-on, 24/7, click-away new technologies have both connected and isolated people, as their capacity for speed cranks up the world's pace.

We describe how the workforce has also changed from what previous generations knew, becoming increasingly diverse, multicultural, dispersed, horizontal, and distributed—and, consequently, requiring more collaboration than competition. We (and other writers) have explored how nationality and culture matter in ways that require greater sensitivity to interpersonal relationships, how the days of a homogeneous workforce are over, and how the newest generation to enter the workforce (the Millennials) place fresh demands on their organizations (but, of course, so did the Gen-Xers, Boomers, and Traditionalists before them).

Bob Dylan's song "The Times They Are A-Changin'" continues to get airtime.

But we also tell them something else. We tell our audiences that as much as the context of leadership has changed, the *content of leadership* has not changed much at all. The fundamental behaviors, actions, and practices of leaders have remained essentially the same since we first began researching and writing about leadership over three decades ago. Much has changed, but there's a whole lot more that's stayed the same.

EVERYONE WANTS TO KNOW THE *TRUTH* ABOUT LEADERSHIP

Initially we set out to write a new book aimed squarely at emerging leaders in the Millennial generation. Millennials are an influential group and on the cusp of replacing Baby Boomers as a game-changing force due to their size and position. Now that Millennials are entering organizations in increasingly large numbers, many leaders with whom we work are sensing a noticeable shift in their workplaces, forcing them to reconsider their leadership practices. They've grown intensely curious about generational differences, and they've kept asking our advice on how they and their young colleagues should lead in these changing times. Since we've worked with college students and young leaders throughout our careers and have had a lot of first-hand experience with generational issues, we thought we could make a contribution to the growing literature on the subject. (And we were more than likely influenced by the fact that we're also parents of Millennials.)

So we did what we've done in the past, as all good researchers and academics do: We conducted a study and gathered data. We brought together several focus groups of Millennials and explored their life experiences, their values, their perspectives on the world, and what they wanted to know about leadership that would better prepare them for their place and responsibility in the world. We expanded our research to include a broader sample of Millennials, and we presented them with the following scenario: "Imagine you're sitting in a meeting with a group of your colleagues. The door to the conference room opens. In walks someone you've never met before, and that person says, 'Hi, I'm your new leader.' What questions immediately come to mind that you want to ask this person?"

As we reviewed the questions Millennials wanted to ask a new leader, an important insight emerged. We found that their concerns and issues were not all that different from those we'd heard from their older sisters and brothers, and even their moms and dads when they'd responded to the same question. They wanted to know what every other generation wanted to know. Age made no difference.

This observation was powerfully reinforced when we analyzed the most current data from the *Leadership Practices Inventory*, our 360-degree leadership assessment tool. Looking at data from over a million respondents, we discovered that age makes no difference in explaining why leaders are effective or ineffective. When it comes to generating positive work attitudes, it doesn't matter whether you're a Traditionalist, a Boomer, a Gen-Xer, or a Millennial. Good leadership is good leadership, regardless of age. It became very apparent once again that the context of leading may change a lot, but the content of leading changes very little.

At about this same time we were deeply honored and humbled to learn that the American Society for Training and Development (ASTD) was going to present us with their annual award for Distinguished Contribution to Workplace Learning and Performance. The award is given, they said, "in recognition of an exceptional contribution of sustained impact to the field of learning and performance." It was presented to us at the 2009 Annual ASTD Conference and Expo, and we were asked to conduct an educational session based on our work. In light of the career-spanning nature of the award, we thought it'd be appropriate to craft a presentation around ideas that we'd been developing, talking about, and writing about since the beginning of our collaboration and research. As we culled through our decades of research, interviews, and data, we found a few kernels of lasting truth, and we entitled our presentation "Enduring Leadership Truths."

As is customary at these kinds of conferences, participants were asked to complete an evaluation of the session. We were a bit nervous about how folks would receive a "retrospective" on our work. After all, this was a group of experienced and seasoned training and development professionals, and sometimes they can be a critical crowd. But we were pleasantly surprised by the feedback we received, particularly the responses to one item. Everyone (yes, 100 percent of the audience) agreed with the statement: "I learned something from this presentation that was new and I can use." To us, these truths were foundational, critical, but not necessarily new. But when presented on their own, without fads or fanfare, leaders and trainers alike found them fresh and useful. It caused us to think that perhaps there was a need for a book that would make a few bold statements about what research has shown to be true about leadership over the years. And that perhaps, when presented in this way, this would be a new and refreshing look at the topic.

We're reminded of a time we shared the platform with renowned leadership educator Ken Blanchard at an association meeting. In the middle of responding to an audience question one of us was saying, "I don't know what you call something that's been the same for twenty-five years, but... ," and Ken interrupted, exclaiming, "I'd call it the truth." It was a moment of clarity. We began to see that we shouldn't be shy about saying that some things about leadership just don't change that much over time, if at all, and that those things need to be understood for what they are—*the truth.*

After the ASTD experience, it became readily apparent to us that we should write a book that focuses not so much on anything new, but rather speaks directly to what endures and is timeless. While context changes, while global and personal circumstances change, the fundamentals of leadership do not. We thought it was just as important in these changing times to remind people of what endures as it was to talk about what has been disrupted.

We wanted to make certain that the lessons we included not only withstood the test of time but also withstood the scrutiny of statistics. So we sifted through the reams of data that had piled up over three decades and isolated those nuggets that were soundly supported by the numbers. This is a collection of the real thing—no fads, no myths, no trendy responses—just truths that endure.

This book reveals the most important things that we've learned since we began our collaboration. It's a collection of fundamental principles that inform and support the practices of leadership. These are lessons that were true thirty years ago, are true today, and we believe will be true thirty years from now. They speak to what the newest and youngest leaders need to appreciate and understand, and they speak just as meaningfully to the oldest leaders, who are perhaps re-purposing themselves as they transition from their lengthy careers to other pursuits in volunteer, community, or public sectors. Entrepreneurs need to appreciate what we have learned, just as do people leading established enterprises. These lessons ring true on athletic fields and in the halls of government, and they make as much sense in the United States, China, Brazil, the European Union, India, or any other global address that you can imagine.

This book does not pretend to be an exhaustive list of everything you ever wanted to know about leadership. There are other truths that we are likely to uncover. In the last two years alone we've analyzed over one million responses to our *Leadership Practices Inventory* from over seventy countries. That's a lot of data points. We've just scratched the surface of our own data, let alone the research from others, and the evidence continues to mount.

For those who have read our prior works, some of this may sound familiar. It should. But three things make this book different from our previous ones. First, this is a bolder book. We're taking a stand that our research supports each and every claim. Second, it's based on data we didn't have when we wrote our other books. Over the past few years we've been able to accumulate a lot more information and a lot more cases. Third, it's a more global and a more cross-generational book. The stories and examples we share come from around the world and encompass three generations of leaders. We know that you'll be the judge, but if you've read our other works we still think you'll find many new and useful insights among these enduring truths.

The truths we've written about in this book are things you can count on. They are realities of leadership that will help you to think, decide, and act more effectively. They provide lessons that will sustain you in your personal and professional development. They are truths that address what is real about leadership.

TEN TRUTHS ABOUT LEADERSHIP

In this book we'll explore ten fundamental truths about leadership and becoming an effective leader. We write with the perspective of an emerging leader—someone new in the role or making the transition to leadership for the first time—but the ideas are just as relevant to those with years of leadership experience. They apply to those who are continuing to hone their skills and to those who've had no prior training. They are also relevant to those who want to be more capable in coaching others to be more effective leaders.

The first truth is that **You Make a Difference**. It is the most fundamental truth of all. Before you can lead, you have to believe that you can have a positive impact on others. You have to believe in yourself. That's where it all begins. Leadership begins when you believe you can make a difference.

The second truth is that **Credibility Is the Foundation of Leadership**. You have to believe in you, but others have to believe in you, too. What does it take for others to believe in you? Short answer: Credibility. We've said it many times, but we need to say it again, especially in these times when people have become cynical about their leaders and institutions: If people don't believe in you, they won't willingly follow you.

The third truth is that **Values Drive Commitment**. People want to know what you stand for and believe in. They want to know what you value. And leaders need to know what others value if they are going to be able to forge alignments between personal values and organizational demands.

The fourth truth is that **Focusing on the Future Sets Leaders Apart**. The capacity to imagine and articulate exciting future possibilities is a defining competence of leaders. You have to take the long-term perspective. Gain insight from reviewing your past and develop outsight by looking around.

You Can't Do It Alone is the fifth truth. No leader ever got anything extraordinary done without the talent and support of others. Leadership is a team sport, and you need to engage others in the cause. What strengthens and sustains the relationship between leader and constituent is that leaders are obsessed with what is best for others, not what is best for themselves.

Trust Rules is the sixth truth. If you can't do it alone and have to rely on others, what's needed to make that happen? Trust. Trust is the social glue that holds individuals and groups together. And the level of trust others have in you will determine the amount of influence you have. You have to earn your constituents' trust before they'll be willing to trust you. That means you have to give trust before you can get trust.

The seventh truth is that **Challenge Is the Crucible for Greatness**. Exemplary leaders—the kind of leaders people want to follow—are always associated with changing the status quo. Great achievements don't happen when you keep things the same. Change invariably involves challenge, and challenge tests you. It introduces you to yourself. It brings you face-to-face with your level of commitment, your grittiness, and your values. It reveals your mindset about change.

Truth number eight reminds you that **You Either Lead by Example or You Don't Lead at All**. Leaders have to keep their promises and become role models for the values and actions they espouse. You have to go first as a leader. You can't ask others to do something you aren't willing to do yourself. Moreover, you have to be willing to admit mistakes and be able to learn from them.

Truth number nine is that **The Best Leaders Are the Best Learners**. You have to believe that you (and others) can learn to lead, and that you can become a better leader tomorrow than you are today. Leaders are constant improvement fanatics, and learning is the master skill of leadership. Learning, however, takes time and attention, practice and feedback, along with good coaching. It also takes willingness on your part to ask for support.

The tenth truth is that **Leadership Is an Affair of the Heart**. It could also be the first truth. Leaders are in love with their constituents, their customers and clients, and the mission that they are serving. Leaders make others feel important and are gracious in showing their appreciation. Love is the motivation that energizes leaders to give so much for others. You just won't work hard enough to become great if you aren't doing what you love.

YOU MATTER

As we do in all of our writings and presentations, we endeavor to make our ideas accessible—easy to understand and simple to translate into action—and we continue to provide encouragement for getting started on the path of becoming a better leader. Doing so begins with you, your desire and commitment. We have never said it would be easy. We both know from our own personal experiences—and humbling ones at times at times—that it is much easier to write about leadership than it is to practice leadership.

This isn't a *"How To"* or *"Made Easy"* or *"For Dummies"* approach to leadership—it is a book about fundamentals. And fundamentals are the necessary building blocks to greatness. You can't fast-track your way to excellence. Leadership is a demanding, noble discipline not to be entered into frivolously or casually. It requires an elevated sense of mastery. And, you can do it. It's a matter of technique, of skill, of practice. It's also a matter of desire and commitment.

There are *enduring* truths about leadership. You can gain mastery over the art and science of leadership by understanding them and attending to them in your workplace and everyday life.

As always, we thank you for taking the time to consider our ideas. We are joined in a common cause with you to increase the quantity and the effectiveness of leaders in the world. The truth is that we need your exemplary leadership now more than ever.

————

James M. Kouzes
Barry Z. Posner
July 2010

YOU MAKE
A DIFFERENCE

Everything you will ever do as a leader is based on one audacious assumption. It's the assumption that *you matter.*

Before you can lead others, you have to lead yourself and believe that you can have a positive impact on others. You have to believe that your words can inspire and your actions can move others. You have to believe that what you do counts for something. If you don't, you won't even try. Leadership begins with you.

The Truth Is That You Make a Difference. It is not a question of "Will I make a difference?" Rather, it's "What difference will I make?" Consider the experience of Melissa Poe.[1]

In 1989 Melissa, then a fourth-grader in Nashville, Tennessee, became very concerned about the natural environment and the kind of world she and her friends might live in if people didn't start paying attention to their everyday actions. After seeing a television program about pollution that portrayed a very scary future, Melissa asked the question, "Will the future be a safe place to live in when I get older?"[2] She decided she had to do something about it. That night she wrote a letter to President George Bush, Sr., asking him to help stop pollution. At the time, Melissa believed the only way to stop pollution was to get everyone involved and that the only way to get everyone involved was to get someone everyone listened to involved.

For twelve weeks she didn't hear back, but Melissa knew the pollution problem wouldn't wait. So she started to do other things to get people's attention. At home Melissa and her family started recycling, turning lights and faucets off when they weren't in use, and planting trees. She wrote more letters to more politicians such as her local mayor, congressmen, and senators. She called up the local television station and did an on-camera commentary. She wrote to her newspaper. She did everything she could think of to help get people's attention.

Melissa also started a club called Kids F.A.C.E. (Kids For a Clean Environment) so that her friends, who'd been asking how they could help, could do projects together like writing letters, planting trees, and picking up litter. "We knew we were doing small things, but we also knew it took a bunch of small things to make a big difference," she told us.

When she still hadn't heard back from the President after several weeks, Melissa, realizing he was a busy man, felt she needed to do more to get him to see her letter. She decided to make her letter bigger so he couldn't miss it. She called a local billboard company in her hometown of Nashville and asked whether they would put a billboard up with her letter to the President. The company donated the billboard to Melissa. However, Melissa knew the President would not see her billboard unless it was in Washington, D.C., where the President lived. Again, she called her local billboard company to ask for help. While they couldn't put up a billboard in Washington, D.C., they were able to connect Melissa to another billboard company that could. In a matter of six months, over 250 billboards were put up all over the United States, including at least one in each state and one just a mile from the White House.

Almost immediately, Melissa began receiving letters from other kids who were as concerned as she was about the environment. They wanted to help. By the time she finally received a response from the President—a disappointing form letter—she no longer needed the help of someone famous to get her message across. Melissa had found within herself the personal power to inspire others to become involved and make a difference.

In January, just six months after she began her journey to get people's attention about the environment, Melissa appeared on the *Today* show to tell her story. It is here that Kids F.A.C.E. grew from a local club to a national organization. Membership swelled. As the organization grew, Melissa's first Kids F.A.C.E. project, a recycling program at her school, led to a manual full of ideas on how to clean up the environment. Then there were other challenges over the years, such as the One in a Million campaign, a successful project that engaged over one million kids to plant one million trees by 2000.

Starting with just six members at her elementary school, Kids F.A.C.E. grew to more than two thousand club chapters in twenty-two countries and more than 350,000 members during the time Melissa was president. (Today there are 500,000 members.) At age seventeen, she stepped aside, joined the board, and handed over the reins to two fifteen-year-olds, saying she was too old for the job. She wanted the organization to always be in kids' hands so that there was always a club for kids and by kids.

WHATEVER YOU NEED YOU ALREADY HAVE

Is Melissa a leader? Can someone at age nine or seventeen demonstrate the practices of exemplary leadership? Aren't those abilities reserved for people mainly in senior positions in big-time organizations?

Yes, yes, and no. Yes, Melissa is a leader. Yes, you can demonstrate leadership at any age. No, leadership is not about some position in an organization and clearly not just for those in senior positions.

Too often images of who's a leader and who's not are all mixed up in preconceived notions about what leadership is and is not. Conventional wisdom portrays leadership as something found mostly at the top. Myth and legend treat leadership as if it were the private reserve of a very few charismatic men and women. Nothing is further from the truth. Leadership is much more broadly distributed in the population, and it's accessible to anyone who has passion and purpose to change the way things are.

Fast-forward now to June 4, 2009, twenty years after Melissa Poe wrote that letter to the President of the United States. On that night Melissa Poe Hood—she's grown up now, graduated from college, married, and is working—received the Women of Distinction Award from the American Association of University Women (AAUW) and the National Association of Student Personnel Administrators (NASPA). In acknowledging the honor, here's the advice she gave the college women student leaders in the audience:

> Change does not begin with someone else. Change
> begins in your own backyard, no matter your
> age or your size. I had no idea that one simple

action could change my life so much. Most
journeys start this way, with simple motivation
and a choice to do something or not. You never
know where one step will take you, and you
never know where the next one will lead. The
difference with being a leader is that you take
the step; you take the journey. The greatest
obstacle you will ever encounter is yourself. Just
like Dorothy never knew that she always had
the ticket home, the Scarecrow always had a
brain, the Tin Man always had a compassionate
heart, even the Cowardly Lion had courage.
Everything you need to be a successful leader
you already have: your intelligence to see an
issue and a way to fix it, your heart to stay
motivated, and your courage not to give up.
You can't look for the man behind the curtain
to solve your concerns. Everything you need
you already have. It's all about taking the
first step.[3]

Melissa's message shines the spotlight on the first
enduring leadership truth. You don't have to look up for
leadership. You don't have to look out for leadership.
You only have to look inward. You have the potential to
lead others to places they have never been before. A nine-
year-old Melissa looked inward and found a leader. You
can do the same. Leadership begins with you.

LEADER ROLE MODELS ARE LOCAL

We've been gathering stories about personal best leadership experiences, including this one from Melissa, for three decades. The people we've talked to come from every type of organization, public and private, government and NGO, high-tech and low-tech, small and large, schools and professional services. They are young and old, male and female, and from every ethnic group. They represent every imaginable vocation and avocation. They reside all over the globe. Leaders are found everywhere. Demographics play no role in whether or not someone is going to become an exemplary leader.

After examining the immense variety of stories from so many different people and places, it has also become crystal clear that leadership is not a birthright. It's not about position or title. It's not about power or authority. It's not about celebrity or wealth. It's not about being a CEO, president, general, or prime minister. It's not about being a superstar. And it's most assuredly not about some charismatic gift.

Over the last couple of years, we analyzed data from over a million people around the globe to assess the practices of leaders. The numbers reveal that the behavior of leaders explains more about why people feel engaged and positive about their workplaces than any particular individual or organizational characteristic. Factors like age, gender, ethnicity, function, position, nationality, organizational size, industry, tenure, and education *together* account for less than 1 percent of the reason that people feel productive, motivated, energized, effective, and committed in their workplaces. The leaders' behaviors, on the other hand, explain nearly 25 percent of the reason.[4] Leadership is not about *who* you are or *where* you come from. It's about *what* you do.

When we first reported on Melissa's story in 1993, we had no idea that in 2009 she'd be a Woman of Distinction. Neither did she. But Melissa knew then, and she knows now, that leadership begins with taking that first step.

Here's something else to consider. For a long time now we've been asking people about the leader role models in their own lives. Not well-known historical leaders, but leaders with whom they've had personal experience. We've asked them to identify the person they'd select as their most important role model for leadership, and then we've given them a list of eight possible categories from which these leaders might come. They can choose from business leader, community or religious leader, entertainer or Hollywood star, family member, political leader, professional athlete, teacher or coach, or other/none/not sure. Take a look at the results.[5]

Data on Leader Role Models

Role Model Category	Respondent Age Category	
	18 to 30	**Over 30**
Family member	40%	46%
Teacher or coach	26%	14%
Community or religious	11%	8%
Business leader	7%	23%
Political leader	4%	4%
Professional athlete	3%	0%
Entertainer	2%	0%
None/not sure/other	7%	4%

Regardless of whether one is under or over thirty years of age, when thinking back over their lives and selecting their most important leader role models, people are more likely to choose a family member than anyone else. Mom and Dad, it turns out, are the most influential leaders after all. In second place, for respondents thirty years of age and under, is a teacher or coach, and the third spot goes to a community or religious leader. For the over-thirty crowd, a business leader is number two. But when we probe further, people tell us that a business leader really means the person who was an immediate supervisor at work, not someone in the C-suite. In third position is a teacher or coach. And in the fourth spot are community and religious leaders.

What do you notice about the top groups on the list? You should notice that they're the people you know well and who know you well. They're the leaders you are closest to and who are closest to you. They're the ones with whom you have the most intimate contact. And they're the people you meet early in your lives. If you're in a role that brings you into contact with young people on a regular basis—say a parent, teacher, coach, or counselor—keep this observation in mind. Someone is looking to you right now for leadership.

Notice also how few people find leader role models among those who get all the media attention. No more than 4 percent look up to politicians, professional athletes, or entertainers as their leader role models. You can't measure leadership in column inches or Google search results. You can't measure it in bling, entourages, or gold medals. You can't measure it in fame or fortune. You measure it by the actions people you know take that cause you to look to them for guidance along the important journeys in your life.

Leader role models are local. You find them close to where you live and work.

YOU ARE THE MOST IMPORTANT LEADER

You also definitely find leader role models "close to home" in your organization. The media, and many leadership gurus, focus a lot of attention on people at the top of organizations—founders, CEOs, generals, presidents, and the like. They make it seem as if these top dogs are the only ones responsible for everything that's great, and everything that's lousy, about organizations. It's a subtle thing, but it perpetuates the trickle-down theory of leadership: all things start at the top and trickle down to the bottom. But, when you actually look at the data, you see a very different picture.

The leader who has the most impact on your day-to-day behavior is, in fact, not the CEO, the COO, the CFO, or any other C—unless, of course, you report directly to that person. The leader who has the most influence over your desire to stay or leave, your commitment to the organization's vision and values, your ethical decisions and actions, your treatment of customers, your ability to do your job well, and the direction of your career, to name but a few outcomes, is your most immediate manager.

We've been tracking the impact leaders have on their constituents and the organization for many years. As we've already mentioned, we've analyzed data from well over a million respondents, and hundreds of other researchers have used our model and the *Leadership Practices Inventory*[6] to gather data from thousands more. The findings from all these studies point to one very clear conclusion: Managers, volunteers, pastors, government administrators, military officers, teachers, school principals, students, and other leaders who use The Five Practices of Exemplary Leadership® are seen more frequently by others as better leaders.

For example, they:

- More successfully meet job-related demands
- More effectively represent their units to upper management
- Create higher-performing teams
- Increase sales and customer satisfaction levels
- Foster renewed loyalty and greater organizational commitment
- Increase motivation and the willingness to work hard
- Facilitate high patient satisfaction scores and meet family member needs
- Promote high degrees of involvement and engagement in schools
- Enlarge the size of their congregations
- Expand fundraising results and gift-giving levels
- Extend the range of their agencies' services
- Reduce absenteeism, turnover, and dropout rates
- Positively influence recruitment rates
- Earn higher scores on measures of leader credibility

Additionally, people working with leaders who demonstrate The Five Practices of Exemplary Leadership® are significantly more satisfied with the actions and strategies of their leaders; they feel more committed, excited, energized, influential, and powerful; and they are more productive. In other words, the more you engage in the practices of exemplary leadership, the more likely it is that you'll have a positive influence on others in the organization.

All this means that, if you're a manager, to your direct reports *you* are the most important leader in the organization. You have much more impact than your CEO on your direct reports' day-to-day performance. And, if that's the case, isn't it your responsibility to be the best leader you can be? You are accountable for the leadership you demonstrate.

THE FIVE PRACTICES OF EXEMPLARY LEADERSHIP®

The Five Practices of Exemplary Leadership is the model of best-practices leadership that emerged from our research.[7] These five "practices" (not "laws" or "principles") are

1. Model the Way
2. Inspire a Shared Vision
3. Challenge the Process
4. Enable Others to Act
5. Encourage the Heart

And even if you are not in a management position, there is really no escape. No matter what your position is, you have to take responsibility for the quality of leadership people experience. No one made Melissa Poe the leader. She took personal responsibility for doing something about a serious problem she recognized and started leading. No one can make you a leader, either. You have to take that first step for yourself. You have to be willing to take actions that others will want to follow.

After all, if you aren't willing to follow yourself, why would anyone else want to?

Also keep in mind that you have the chance to truly change a life. As the author Marianne Williamson has written:

> Our deepest fear is not that we are inadequate. Our deepest fear is that we are powerful beyond measure. It is our light, not our darkness that most frightens us.... Your playing small does not serve the world. There is nothing enlightened about shrinking so that other people won't feel insecure around you.... And as we let our own light shine, we unconsciously give other people permission to do the same. As we are liberated from our own fear, our presence automatically liberates others.[8]

You have the chance to make the world a better place as a result of what you do. What could be more rewarding than that?

———

The Truth Is That You Make a Difference. Somewhere, sometime, the leader within you may get the call to step forward—for the school, the congregation, the community, the agency, the company, the union, or the family. By believing in yourself and in your capacity to lead, you open yourself to hearing the call. You open yourself to making a difference in the world.

CREDIBILITY IS THE FOUNDATION OF LEADERSHIP

L eadership begins with you and your belief in yourself. Leadership continues only if other people also believe in you.

All the programs to develop leaders, all the courses and classes, all the books and tapes, all the blogs and websites offering tips and techniques are meaningless unless the people who are supposed to follow believe in the person who's supposed to lead.

The Truth Is That Credibility Is the Foundation of Leadership. This is the inescapable conclusion we've come to after thirty years of asking people around the world what they look for and admire in a leader, someone whose direction they would *willingly* follow. The key word in the preceding sentence is "willingly." It's one thing to follow someone because you think you have to "or else," and it's another when you follow a leader because you want to. What does it take to be the kind of person, the kind of leader, others want to follow, doing so enthusiastically and voluntarily?

It turns out that the believability of the leader determines whether people will willingly give more of their time, talent, energy, experience, intelligence, creativity, and support. Only credible leaders earn commitment, and only commitment builds and regenerates great organizations and communities.

CONSTITUENTS HAVE CLEAR EXPECTATIONS OF THEIR LEADERS

Leadership is a relationship between those who aspire to lead and those who choose to follow. You can't have one without the other. Leadership strategies, tactics, skills, and practices are empty without an understanding of the fundamental dynamics of this relationship.

In every relationship people have expectations of each other. Sometimes these expectations are clearly voiced, and other times they're never discussed, but nonetheless expectations are present in every human relationship. In 1980 we became curious about what constituents expected from their leaders. Most of the leadership literature talked about what leaders expected of their followers, but we wanted to know what followers expected of their leaders. We wanted to know the values, personal traits, or characteristics people looked for and admired in someone they would be willing to follow.[1] Since that time we've surveyed tens of thousands of people around the world asking them to select the qualities that they most wanted in a leader.

Year after year the results of our research have been striking in their regularity. And year after year they do not vary significantly by demographical, organizational, or cultural dimensions. It has become quite clear, as the data in the table below illustrates, that there are a few essential "character tests" someone (you) must pass before others are willing to grant the designation of leader.

Characteristics of Admired Leaders

*Percentage of Respondents Selecting
Each Characteristic*

Characteristic	Percentage Selecting
Honest	85
Forward-Looking	70
Inspiring	69
Competent	64
Intelligent	42
Broad-Minded	40

(continued)

Characteristics of Admired Leaders (*continued*)

Percentage of Respondents Selecting Each Characteristic

Characteristic	Percentage Selecting
Dependable	37
Supportive	36
Fair-Minded	35
Straightforward	31
Determined	28
Cooperative	26
Ambitious	26
Courageous	21
Caring	20
Loyal	18
Imaginative	18
Mature	16
Self-Controlled	11
Independent	6

Note: We asked each respondent to select seven characteristics out of twenty, so the total percentage adds up to more than 100 percent. These percentages represent respondents from six continents: Africa, North America, South America, Asia, Europe, and Australia. The majority of respondents are from the United States.

Although every characteristic received some votes, and therefore each is important to some people, what is most striking and most evident is that only four qualities have continuously received an average of over 60 percent of the votes. Before anyone is going to willingly follow you—or any other leader—he or she wants to know that you are *honest, forward-looking, inspiring,* and *competent.* Before they are going to voluntarily heed your advice, take your direction, accept your guidance, trust your judgment, agree to your recommendations, buy your products, support your ideas, and implement your strategies, people expect that you will measure up to these criteria. And our research documents this consistent pattern across countries, cultures, ethnicities, organizational functions and hierarchies, gender, and educational and age groups.

But what do these criteria really mean?

Being honest means telling the truth and having ethical principles and clear standards by which you live. People need to believe that your character and integrity are solid. They need to believe that you are worthy of their trust. To be honest with others also requires being honest with yourself and taking stock of what is truly important to you. It means understanding what stirs your personal passion and what's worth making painful sacrifices for. You have to be candid with yourself about your strengths and limitations. You have to know in your heart that you truly believe what you are saying.

Being forward-looking means having a sense of direction and a concern for the future of the organization.

Whether it's called a vision, a mission, or a personal agenda, the message is clear: You must know where you're going if you expect others to willingly join you on the journey. But it's not just *your* vision that others care to know. They also expect that you'll be able to connect your image of the future to *their* hopes, dreams, and aspirations. People won't willingly follow you until they can see how they share in the future you envision.

Being inspiring means sharing the genuine enthusiasm, excitement, and energy you have about the exciting possibilities ahead. People expect you to be positive, upbeat, and optimistic. Your energy signals your personal commitment, and your optimism signals your hope. Others need you to encourage them to reach higher, engage more fully, and put forth greater effort. They need to see and feel your passion for the cause. After all, if you display little or no passion, why should anyone else? If you want others to voluntarily engage in challenging pursuits, then you have to uplift your constituents' spirits. You have to give them reason to believe that tomorrow will be even better than today.

Being competent refers to your track record and your ability to get things done. People have to believe that you know what you are talking about and that you know what you are doing. They want to be confident that you have the skills and abilities to follow through on the promises that you make, but also that you have the self-confidence to admit that you don't know something but are capable of learning. Competence inspires confidence that you will be able to guide the enterprise, large or small, in the direction in which it needs to go.

Leadership competence is different from technical competence. You don't have to be the most skilled engineer to lead a high-technology company, for instance, but you do need to be able to mobilize the best efforts of your engineers to get extraordinary things done.

Being honest, forward-looking, inspiring, and competent are the qualities that the majority of your constituents look for in you. They are at the core of others' expectations. They are the basic measures of whether others will consider you to be the leader they'd willingly follow.

CREDIBILITY TIES IT ALL TOGETHER

These four characteristics of admired leaders—being honest, forward-looking, inspiring, and competent—have remained constant over more than thirty years of economic growth and decline; the surge in new technology enterprises; the birth of the World Wide Web; the further globalization of business and industry; the ever-changing political environment; the expansion bursting and re-generation of the Internet economy; three wars; and the worst recession since the Great Depression. The relative importance of the most desired qualities has varied somewhat over time, but there has been no change in the fact that these are the four qualities people want most in their leaders.

This list of four consistent findings is useful in and of itself. You can use it in selection, recruitment, orientation, assessment, and retention of leaders. You can use it for your own development. You can use it when you go to the polling booth to vote. But there's a more profound implication revealed by this research.

Three of these four key characteristics make up what communications experts refer to as "source credibility." In assessing the believability of sources of communication— whether from newscasters, salespeople, physicians, priests, business managers, military officers, politicians, or civic leaders—researchers typically evaluate them on three criteria: their perceived trustworthiness, expertise, and dynamism. Those who are rated more highly on these dimensions are considered to be more credible sources of information.[2]

Notice how strikingly similar these three characteristics are to the essential leader qualities of honest, competent, and inspiring—three of the top four items selected in our research. We've found in our investigation of admired leadership qualities that, more than anything, people want to follow leaders who are credible. Credibility is the foundation of leadership. (Indeed, this is so fundamental to understanding the effectiveness of leaders that we've even written an entire book on it![3])

Above all else, people must be able to believe in their leaders. They must believe that your word can be trusted, that you are personally passionate and enthusiastic about the work that you're doing, and that you have the necessary knowledge and skill to lead.

In addition to the three factors that measure source credibility, the vast majority of constituents have one other expectation of leaders. They expect leaders to be forward-looking. People must also believe that you know where you are headed and have a vision for the future. Being forward-looking sets leaders apart from other credible people, and it also makes personal credibility even more important to leaders.

Compared to other sources of information (for example, news anchors), leaders do more than reliably report the news. Leaders make the news and interpret the news. This makes your job as a leader different from those in the role of individual contributor. People in other roles are not expected to be forward-looking, but you are. As a leader, you are expected to have a point of view about the future. You are expected to articulate exciting possibilities about how today's work will result in tomorrow's world.

This expectation that you should be forward-looking reveals how important it is for you to be diligent in building and sustaining your personal credibility. Your ability to take strong stands, to challenge the status quo, and to point people in new directions depends on just how credible you are. If you are highly credible, people are much more likely to enlist in your campaign for the future. But if others don't believe in you, then the message you are delivering about an uplifting and ennobling future rests on a weak and precarious foundation. People may actually applaud your vision of the future but be unwilling to follow you in that direction. They may agree that what you are saying needs to be done, but they just won't have the faith and confidence that you are the one to lead them there. We refer to this principle as The Kouzes-Posner First Law of Leadership:

If you don't believe in the messenger, you won't believe the message.

CREDIBILITY MATTERS

At this point, you might very well say, "So what? I know someone who is in a position of power, or I know people who are enormously wealthy, and I don't find them credible. Does credibility really matter? Does it make a difference?" It's a legitimate concern, so we empirically studied the question of whether or not credibility matters in leading others to get extraordinary things done.

Because our concern is everyday leadership, we decided to ask questions about leaders who are close to home. While it's great sport to explore the credibility of top management, elected officials, or other highly visible leaders, we wanted to know more about how credibility influenced the work of the average person in a typical organization. So we asked people to think about the actions of their immediate managers when responding to our survey questions. We asked organization members to rate their immediate managers on the extent to which they exhibited credibility-enhancing behaviors, and then we asked the respondents to indicate how they felt about certain aspects of their work and their organizations.

In these studies we find that when people say their immediate manager exhibits high credibility, they're significantly more likely to: be proud to tell others they're part of the organization, feel a strong sense of team spirit, see their own personal values as consistent with those of the organization, feel attached and committed to the organization, and have a sense of ownership of the organization. On the other hand, when people say their manager exhibits low credibility they're significantly more likely to produce only if they are watched carefully, are motivated primarily by money, say good things about the organization publicly but criticize it privately, consider looking for another job if the organization experiences problems, and feel unsupported and unappreciated.

James Stout, an international MBA student, underscored these findings when he summed up the conclusion he came to after interviewing the leader he most admires. He told us that he realized leadership was a reciprocal relationship. Regardless of level, people look for the same qualities in leaders, he observed. The expectations go both ways, and you get what you expect. "Consequently," he said, "leaders at the highest levels greatly influence the development of leadership in their organizations by demonstrating qualities that set the tone for emerging leaders." If leaders in the most senior positions live up to the exemplary standards, he observed, "the organization experiences a constant elevation of strong leadership as senior leaders pull their constituents upward toward similar standards." A culture of leadership excellence and integrity is created when people at all levels genuinely expect each other to be credible, and they hold each other accountable for the actions that build and sustain credibility.

Credibility makes the difference between being an effective leader and being an ineffective one. Credibility will determine whether others want to follow you or not. You must take this personally. The loyalty, commitment, energy, and productivity of your constituents depend on it. And the effect of personal integrity of leaders goes far beyond employee attitudes. It also influences customer and investor loyalty. People are just more likely to stick with you when they know they are dealing with a credible person and a credible institution. In business, and in life, if people don't believe in you, they won't stand by you.

BELIEVE IT WHEN YOU SEE IT

The data confirms that credibility is the foundation of leadership. But what is credibility behaviorally? How do you know it when you see it?

In asking this question worldwide, the answer we heard is essentially the same, regardless of how it may be phrased in one company versus another or one country versus another. The universally common refrain is "They do what they say they will do."

Arthur Taute, a registered professional engineer and most recently CEO of Vela VKE (South Africa), said: "Leadership means being absolutely honest and helping others to do as I do, not simply to do what I say." Credibility, as Arthur points out, doesn't come from giving orders; it comes from aligning your actions and your words. Indeed, when it comes to deciding whether a leader is believable, you first listen to the words, but then you watch his or her actions. You listen to the talk, and then watch the walk. For example, you hear the promises of resources to support change initiatives, and then you wait to see whether the money and materials follow. A judgment of "credible" is handed down when words and deeds are consonant.

This realization leads to a straightforward prescription for establishing credibility. It's The Kouzes-Posner Second Law of Leadership:

DWYSYWD, or Do What You Say You Will Do.

This is precisely what Wesley Lord learned from his own personal best leadership experience as the coxswain for the local rowing club. "I would never ask them to do something I wouldn't be willing to do myself," he told us. "They knew that if I asked them for something that I would be willing to the same if they asked me."

———

The Truth Is That Credibility Is the Foundation of Leadership. If you are going to lead, you must have a relationship with others that is responsive to their expectations that you are someone they can believe in. If people are going to willingly follow you, it is because they believe you are credible. To be credible in action, you must do what you say you will do. That means that you must be so clear about your beliefs that you can put them into practice every day. The consistent living out of values is a behavioral way of demonstrating honesty and trustworthiness. It proves that you believe in the path you have taken and are progressing forward with energy and determination. We'll explore both of these expectations more fully in other chapters in this book.

VALUES DRIVE
COMMITMENT

Imagine you're sitting in a meeting with a group of your colleagues. The door to the conference room opens and in walks someone you've never met before who says, "Hi, I'm your new leader." What questions immediately come to mind that you want to ask this person?

We presented this scenario in the introduction and use it regularly as part of our ongoing leadership research. People have lots of questions they would want to ask, but by far the most frequently asked is: "Who are you?"

People want to know your values and beliefs, what you really care about, and what keeps you awake at night. They want to know who most influenced you, the events that shaped your attitudes, and the experiences that prepared you for the job. They want to know what drives you, what makes you happy, and what ticks you off. They want to know what you're like as a person and why you want to be their leader. They want to know whether you play an instrument, compete in sports, go to the movies, or enjoy the theater. They want to know about your family, what you've done, and where you've traveled. They want to understand your personal story. They want to know why they ought to be following you.

So if you are the new leader who walks into that room one day, you'd better be prepared to answer the "Who are you?" question. And to answer that question for others, you first have to answer it for yourself. In one of our leadership workshops, our colleague Spencer Clark explained himself to students in the following way:

> I am the chief learning officer for Cadence Design
> Systems. I was a division president for Black &
> Decker and a general manager for General Electric.
> But these [job titles] are not who I am. If you want
> to know who I am, you need to understand that I
> grew up in Kentucky. That I was one of four sons,
> and we lived on a sharecropper's farm and slept in
> a home that had no inside plumbing. Who I am is
> not simply what I do. Knowing who I am has been
> enormously helpful in guiding me in making deci-
> sions about what I would do and how I would do it.

As Spencer makes clear, his job resume says very little about who he is and why he makes the decisions he makes and takes the actions he takes. He knows that there is far more to him than his work history, the titles he's had, and the positions he's held. In order for Spencer to become the leader that he is, he had to dig beneath the surface and find out more about those events that shaped him, the beliefs that informed him, and the values that guided him. He also knows that it's helpful for others to understand those same things before they can commit to his leadership decisions and actions.

What's true for Spencer is true for you. Before you can effectively lead others, you have to understand who you are, where you come from, and the values that guide you.

The Truth Is That Values Drive Commitment. You cannot fully commit to something that isn't important to you—no one can. You can't fully commit to something that doesn't fit with who you are and how you see yourself. In order to devote the time, to expend the energy, and to make the sacrifices necessary, you have to know exactly what makes it worth doing in the first place.

In one of our workshops, Olivia Lai told us that she was initially a little taken aback when we asked her to write about her personal best leadership experience: "Here I am, at twenty-five years of age, with four years of work experience. How could I possibly have a personal best in leadership?" After further reflection, she realized that,

> It wasn't all that hard to figure out what my personal best was and write about it. Even more surprising is that it became clear that leadership is everywhere, it takes place every day, and leadership can come from anyone. It doesn't matter that you don't have the title of "manager," "director," "CEO," to go with it. In the end, that's all they are . . . titles on business cards and company directories. Being a true leader transcends all that.
>
> Becoming a leader is a process of internal self-discovery. In order for me to become a leader and become an even better leader, it's important that I first define my values and principles. If I don't know what my own values are and determine expectations for myself, how can I set expectations for others? How will I convey confidence, strong will, and empathy? Without looking within myself, it's not possible for me to look at others and to recognize their potential and help others become leaders.

Through her own process of self-discovery, Olivia, like Spencer, realized one of the most fundamental lessons on learning to lead. Becoming a leader begins when you come to understand who you are, what you care about, and why you do what you do. This is a journey that all leaders must take.

Your ultimate success in business and in life depends on how well you know yourself, what you value, and why you value it. The better you know who you are and what you believe in, the better you are at making sense of the often incomprehensible and conflicting demands you receive daily. Do this, or do that. Buy this, buy that. Decide this, decide that. Support this, support that. You need internal guidance to navigate the turbulent waters in this stormy world. A clear set of personal values and beliefs is the critical controller in that guidance system.

LISTEN TO YOUR INNER SELF

Another one of the emerging leaders we interviewed told us exactly why it's so important to be clear about your beliefs. "You have to understand what you really believe deeply," she said. "People won't follow you, or even pay much attention to you, if you don't have any strong beliefs."

She explained to us in very personal and poignant ways how she had grown up in a culture that stereotyped women and devalued them. For a long time she had, as she phrased it, "ignored my heart and didn't listen to my own voice." But as she engaged in her own leadership development she began to . . .

> . . . understand that everyone has beliefs and values, and that in order for people to lead they've got to connect with them and be able to express

them. This means that I have to let people know
and understand what my thoughts are so that I can
become a good leader. How can others follow me
if I'm not willing to listen to my own inner self?
Now, I let others know what I think is important
and how hard I'm willing to fight for my values.

If you are ever to become a leader whom others
willingly follow, you must be known as someone who
stands by his or her principles. But, as Spencer, Olivia,
and other leaders have discovered for themselves, first
you have to listen to your inner self in order to find them.
There are a lot of different interests out there competing
for your time, your attention, and your approval. Before
you listen to those voices, you have to listen to that
voice inside that tells you what's truly important. Only
then will you know when to say "yes" and when to say
"no"... and mean it.

Values represent the core of who you are. They
influence every aspect of your life: your moral judgments,
the people you trust, the appeals you respond to, the way
you invest your time and your money. And in turbulent
times they provide a source of direction amid all the
depressing news and challenging personal adversities.

Early on in our research, we had the chance to
interview Arlene Blum, the leader of the first all-women's
team to ascend Annapurna. Climbing mountains is clearly

a challenging, often treacherous undertaking, so she ought to know what it takes to stay motivated when times get tough. In these kinds of difficult circumstances, Arlene says, "As long as you believe what you're doing is meaningful, you can cut through the fear and exhaustion and take the next step." It takes more than toughness to keep going when the going gets tough. It's also vital that you find purpose and significance in what you do.

This is a lesson all leaders must learn. To act with integrity, you must first see clearly. Just as sunlight burns away the morning fog, the more light you shine on what you stand for, what you believe in, and what you care about, the more clearly you'll see those road signs pointing in the direction you want to go. Clarity of values gives you the confidence to take the right turns, to make the tough decisions, to act with determination, and to take charge of your life.

YOU COMMIT TO WHAT FITS

It's vitally important that you understand the power of personal values clarity. It's important to your individual effectiveness, your leadership effectiveness, and the effectiveness of those you lead. There is a significant measurable impact on people's performance when values are personally clear. Take a look at Figure 3.1 and see what we discovered.[1]

Figure 3.1 The Impact of Values
Clarity on Commitment

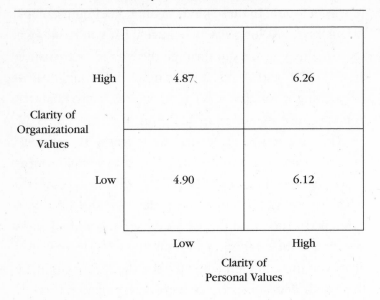

Along the vertical axis is the extent to which people report being clear about their organization's values. Along the horizontal axis is the extent to which these same people report being clear about their own personal values. We correlated these responses with the extent to which people said they were committed to the organization as measured on a scale of 1 (low) to 7 (high). We've organized the data into four cells, each representing a level of clarity from low to high on personal and organizational values. The numbers in each of the four cells represent the level of commitment people have to their organizations as it relates to the degree of their clarity about personal and organizational values.

Notice the quadrant in which people feel the most committed. It's the upper right, with a score of 6.26— high clarity about organizational values and high clarity about personal values. Not surprising. We'd all expect that. Now notice the lowest level of commitment. It's high clarity about organizational values, low clarity about personal—4.87. Actually, that score is not statistically significant from the low-low quadrant—4.90. Finally, look at where the second-highest level of commitment is with a score of 6.12. It's low clarity about organizational values but high clarity about personal values.

At first, this was somewhat jarring to us. You can see that the impact of being very clear or not about the organization's values doesn't seem to make much difference in how committed people are to their organizations. But notice what happens when people are clear on their personal values. First, they are significantly more committed to their organizations, and second, their commitment is not affected by the extent to which they are clear about the organization's values. There is no statistically significant difference in the responses of those high on both versus those only high on personal values clarity.

What does all this mean? Essentially, clarity about personal values has the most significant impact on employees' feelings about their work and what they're doing in the workplace. This is not to say that shared values don't matter. Our research and that of others suggests that they do. People want to be part of something bigger than themselves. What it does say, however, is that people cannot commit fully to anything unless it fits with their own beliefs.

In response to a question about the important leadership lessons he learned over his career, Unilever CEO Paul Polman said, "If your values, your personal values, are aligned with the company's values, you're probably going to be more successful longer term than if they are not. If they are not, it requires you to be an actor when you go to work or to be a split personality."[2] Being an actor or having a split personality aren't on the list of attributes of a credible leader, so making sure that your values and the organization's values are aligned is essential to maintaining your integrity.

DISCOVER WHAT MATTERS

Elaine Fortier, a Silicon Valley veteran, has experienced the ups and downs, booms and busts of the world of high technology. When we interviewed her, she made the following observation about dealing with the challenges she faced during one of the worst downturns in the economy, "Yes, it's tough right now, but it's all part of the adventure. The pioneers crossed the Rocky Mountains in covered wagons, so this is really a walk in the park, isn't it?" Then she went on to tell us about her own personal challenges and the evolution of her philosophy of leadership. "I realized that there was no magic that was going to happen, she told us. "It was now up to me to decide, 'What's my framework for living?'" After over three decades of leadership research, we can say with absolute certainty that Elaine is one-hundred percent correct—you have to decide what matters to you.

The very first step on your leadership development journey is to search for your answer to the question, "What's my framework for living?" You have to find your own true voice. You cannot speak in someone else's. You have to speak in your own. You cannot ask someone else to choose your values for you. You have to choose them for yourself.

Finding your voice is not like finding your keys. You don't just go looking for it by rummaging through the drawers in your house and hoping it'll turn up. English-born poet and organizational consultant David Whyte has written that the "voice throws us back on what we want for our life. It forces us to ask ourselves Who is speaking? Who came to work today? Who is working for what? What do I really care about?"[3]

What do you really care about? Is it success, wealth, family, freedom, growth, love, power, spirituality, trust, wisdom, health, honesty? None of these? All of these? Other values? In the English language there are between 150 and 250 words that represent values, depending on whose research you follow. None of us can be guided by all of them, so we have to make some choices. Which five, six, or seven of these many possibilities best speak to your strongly held and enduring beliefs? Which serve as your guides in making decisions about which job to take or which organization to join? Which enable you to make the tough calls on things like completing the important work project or attending your child's school play?

There's an exercise in our workshops in which we give participants a set of values cards.[4] Much like a deck of playing cards, each card has only one value written on it. We ask everyone to go through the deck, picking out the cards with values that are most meaningful to them, eventually choosing fifteen. Once they have those in front of them, we ask them to further narrow that list down to their top five values. It forces each person to weigh each value in comparison to all the others. While all are valid (and there are no wrong answers), people see for themselves how their own system of values comes together. Reactions run the gamut of emotions, but everyone who has gone through this exercise gains greater clarity about the values that should guide their actions and decisions.

Consider what Sharon Neoh, consultant at Accenture, told us she learned when we challenged her to think about her values:

> I was quite bothered [at first]. . . . I had never before
> asked myself when I had last demonstrated one

of the values I had circled and found it difficult
to find those situations. I came to the realization
that I did not have a clear perspective on my list of
values. That night, I went back home and looked
over the list again and tried to think of situations
where I had demonstrated any one of those values
and asked myself over and over again whether that
was something important to me.

This exercise helped me identify values that
were important to me. What I can do is identify
the values that are important to me and try
my best to act consistently against that set of
values, understanding that they may evolve in the
future as I grow, mature, and experience more
of life.

Take the time, like Sharon and Elaine did, to discover
and identify the values that matter and should guide your
decisions and actions.

IT'S NOT JUST YOUR VALUES

As important as it is that you forthrightly articulate the
principles for which you stand, by no means does this
suggest that your job is then to get other people to
comply with what you say. You are a leader, remember, not a dictator. Leading others is definitely not about
getting others to conform to your point of view. Con-
formity produces compliance, not commitment. Unity is

essential, and unity is forged, not forced. Carlo Argiolas, with Medtronic in Italy, explained to us:

> The first step is to make clear your own personal values and the second step is to listen to others and to observe others in order to understand their values and aspirations. The last step is to communicate and paint a vision that everyone in the proper context can recognize as his or her own vision.

The data showing that personal values drive commitment is just as true for your constituents as it is for you. You can't commit everyone to a list that you came up with in private and then expect them to enthusiastically endorse it. What you espouse, as Carlo points out, must resonate with the aspirations of others. People won't fully commit to the group and organization if they don't sense a good fit with who they are and what they believe.

There seems to be this myth about leadership that what you are supposed to do is ascend the mountain, gain enlightenment, descend with the tablets, and then proclaim the truth to your followers. Nothing could be more damaging to the work of a leader. Leadership is more often about listening than telling. Your task is to gain consensus on a common cause and a common set of principles. You need to build and affirm a community of shared values.

———

The Truth Is That Values Drive Commitment. You can only fully commit to organizations and other causes when there is a good fit between what you value and what the organization values. That means that to do your best as a leader you need to know who you are and what you care about. You need a set of values that guide your decisions and actions. To discover who you are and what you care about, you need to spend some time on the inner work of a leader—in reflection on finding your voice. And keep in mind that it's not just your values that matter. What is true for you is true for others: they too must find a fit with who they are and what they value. Credible leaders listen, not just to their own aspirations, but also to the needs and desires of others. Leadership is a relationship, and relationships are built on mutual understanding.

FOCUSING
ON THE FUTURE
SETS LEADERS APART

We've all had a glimpse of the future. You know, that time when you imagined running your own business, or that dream of traveling to an exotic place, or that bold idea for a game-changing new product, or that burning desire to earn an advanced degree, or that sense of purpose you felt when you signed up for the sustainability campaign, or that calling to join a cause and make this a better planet, or that uplifting sense you had when picturing kids playing in a neighborhood without fear. All of us dream of what might come to pass some day.

Leaders take these dreams seriously and act to make them happen. Remember that scenario about the new leader walking into the room and announcing that she was our new leader? The first question people had was, "Who are you?" The second-most-common question people want an answer to is: "What's your vision?"

People do not have this question for their teammates. It's a question reserved for leaders. People want to know where you're going. They want to know the kind of future you have in mind.

The Truth Is That Focusing On the Future Sets Leaders Apart. The capacity to imagine and articulate exciting future possibilities is the defining competence of leaders. Leaders are custodians of the future. They are concerned about tomorrow's world and those who will inherit it. They ask, "What's new? What's next? What's going to happen after the current project is completed?" They think beyond what's directly in front of them, peer into the distance, imagine what's over the horizon, and move forward toward a new and compelling future.

As you make the transition to leading, keep in mind that your constituents want to know your hopes, your dreams, and your vision. They want to know where you plan to take them. They want to share in that glimpse of the future.

LEADERS LOOK LONG-TERM

Having surveyed thousands of people on what they want in their leaders, in someone they would *willingly* follow, the quality of being *forward-looking* is second only to being *honest* as their most admired leader quality.

On average, 70 percent of respondents select it. In Asia, Europe, and Australia, the preference for forward-looking is several percentage points higher than it is in the United States.

We've also asked a similar question about what people look for in their colleagues (someone you would like on your team) and the responses to this question have revealed a telling and vital distinction between leaders and individual contributors. Using the identical list of desirable qualities, the number one requirement of a leader, being *honest,* was also the top-ranking attribute of a good colleague. But, the second-most-desirable quality of a leader—being *forward-looking*—was nowhere near the top of the list for colleagues. In fact, forward-looking was not even in the top ten attributes of a colleague. It was selected by only 27 percent of the respondents, whereas 70 percent of those same respondents wanted it in a leader. That's a difference of 43 percentage points! No other quality we've studied showed such a dramatic difference between leader and colleague.

Moreover, we found, not surprisingly, that the importance of being forward-looking increased with age, work experience, and level in the organizational hierarchy. For example, while only about one-third of undergraduate college students ranked forward-looking among their most important attributes, over 90 percent of senior executives had it on their lists.

In a related study we found that the desirability of thinking about legacies—an extension of being forward-looking—is important to the majority of managers at every level but becomes even more important as you move up the ladder of responsibility. Younger leaders, however, rarely stop to reflect on their long-term contributions to society and the workplace. They're much more concerned about the present.

What is the difference between being present-oriented and being future-oriented, and why is it so important for leaders? Take, for example, Angela Gu, when she was in her first year as assistant controller, overseeing the accounts payable function in Finance for Wal-Mart China. While Wal-Mart had opened eleven stores in six cities across China, they had expansion plans to triple the store count and enter into more new cities over the following three years. At that time the Finance Department was set up by city, and Angela could see that if the accounts payable function grew at the same rate as the company expanded they would grow from about two hundred people to over eight hundred people within a few years. She told us how she imagined the challenges and problems this would create for her area, "including the people management, procedural control and compliance, and costs related to personnel, travel, training, and telecommunications."

Anticipating the future challenges the company would face, Angela proposed an alternative to the CFO— a centralization initiative—and received approval to move ahead. The program involved all divisions in the home office and local cities, including human resources, merchandising, and operations, in addition to finance. The effort paid off almost immediately in terms of productivity, improved control, and standardization, and established a platform for future efficiency-driven programs. Within a year the average number of accounts payable associates serving one store was reduced by 40 percent, and within three years, the actual headcount in accounts payable had been reduced by nearly 50 percent, despite the almost four-fold expansion of new stores. Angela explains:

> The initiative was quite new, with no other precedent to refer to, but the vision of a national accounts payable center excited me. You can always choose to follow whatever you have been doing—which demands from you no extra thinking or efforts—or you can focus on accomplishing something different which would do good for the enterprise.

Being forward-looking paid dividends for Angela and for Wal-Mart. This kind of anticipatory thinking can do the same for you.

YOU HAVE TO SPEND MORE TIME IN THE FUTURE

The challenge for young and aspiring leaders, like Angela, is to envision the future. Just as she did, you have to look beyond what's in front of you and imagine the exciting possibilities that the future holds. Yet, in spite of the fact that *being forward-looking* is the quality that most separates leaders from individual contributors, it's something that too few fully appreciate and that too many devote almost no time to developing.

If nothing is done to address this shortcoming, it will become a huge barrier to your future success. That's because the challenge escalates with managerial level. Front-line leaders are expected to anticipate events only about three months down the road. Due to the timelines of their more complex projects, middle-level managers often need to look three to five years into the future. Those in the executive suite must focus on a horizon that's ten or more years away. For example, the president of a division of an aerospace company told us he was bidding on a project that wouldn't be completed for eighteen years. If you're held hostage to the present, there's no way you'll be free to lead others to destinations that can't be reached for many years.

Crossing the chasm from individual contributor to leader requires fully embracing the need to develop the capacity to envision the future. Making the transition from average to exemplary leader, regardless of level, requires the dedication to master it.[1]

And how does a new leader develop the capacity to be forward-looking? The answer is deceptively simple: *spend more time in the future.* You have to carve out more time each week to peering into the distance and imagining what might be out there. You have to spend the time today in order to have the time tomorrow.

Sounds simple, right? All you have to do is spend time thinking deliberately about the future—anywhere from thirty minutes to a couple of hours a day, depending on your level. The trouble is, it's not all that easy to do. Even the most experienced and senior executives struggle with it.

Here's a dose of reality: Researchers tell us that most top executives spend only about 3 percent of their time thinking about, and getting others on board with, the critical issues that will shape their business ten or more years down the road.[2] That's not nearly enough time. That's why you have to be disciplined about this.

Michael Hyatt, CEO of the publishing company Thomas Nelson, writes in his blog about why it's so important for leaders to spend the time to create a compelling vision of the future:

> Vision is the lifeblood of any organization. It is
> what keeps it moving forward. It provides meaning

to the day-to-day challenges and setbacks that make
up the rumble and tumble of real life.

Michael then goes on to talk about how in tough
economic times things get very tactical and focused
on survival and how decisions become very pragmatic.
After a while this short-term approach grinds us down.
People lose sight of the bigger picture. Michael points
out that:

> This is where great leadership makes all the dif-
> ference. Leadership is more than influence. It is
> about reminding people of what it is we are trying
> to build—and why it matters. It is about paint-
> ing a picture of a better future. It comes down
> to pointing the way and saying, "C'mon. We can
> do this!"[3]

It is your job as a leader to lift people's sights and lift
people's spirits. You must remind others, who are often
so mired in the day-to-day details of work and life that
they lose their bearings, that there is a larger purpose to
all this doing. You and they are working hard in order
to build something different, to make something new, to
create a better future. You are here to make a difference
in the world. That's why it's important to invest the time
today in tomorrow's future.

INSIGHT: EXPLORE YOUR PAST EXPERIENCE

As surprising as it might seem, in aiming for the future you need to look back into your past. Looking backward can actually enable you to see farther than if you stare straight ahead. You also enrich your future and give it detail as you recall the richness of your past experiences. This was precisely the lesson realized by Jade Lui, recruitment consultant with Ambition Group, who told us that: "In order to look into the future I first needed to search my past for recurring life-long themes. This gives me clarity on identifying the big picture but also understanding current trends." For younger leaders it may be more difficult to look back—there's just less past to recall—but it's still important at any age to think about those repeating themes in your life, those messages you keep getting about what matters most.

Your central theme in life more than likely wasn't something that just occurred to you this morning. It's been there for a long time. You may not have ever explored your past for a persistent and repeating ideal, but if you were to examine the recurring theme in your life, what might you find? What's been that topic you keep coming back to again and again? What's been that story you keep telling and retelling? For some it might be a concern for a healthy environment that keeps repeating itself. For others it might be open computer architecture, self-managed investing, the wireless Web, e-commerce, virtual learning, fair housing, affordable health care, safe schools, religious freedom, equal rights, global warming, or any number of possibilities. Search your past to find that theme.

In addition to identifying themes in your life, there's another benefit to looking back before looking ahead: You can gain a greater appreciation for how long it can take to fulfill your aspirations. There are many, many avenues for you to pursue. Indeed, there may actually be no end in sight. In your life you may have many dreams—and probably several that have no endings, but are noble aspirations to always be pursuing.

OUTSIGHT: IMAGINE THE POSSIBILITIES

Joe Fox, along with his older brother Avi, has been the founder of two industry-changing companies. Their first company was a pioneering online brokerage called Web Street, which was acquired by E-Trade Group in the early 2000s. Joe believes that you can't force innovation and that you have to "observe the world with a fresh eye."[4] He describes how he got others to see the possibility that he saw, given the challenge of explaining something that had never existed before:

> I always use a pad of paper to lay out my five-year vision. With Web Street, I sketched the concept by drawing a computer screen—what you'll see on it, what advantages it will offer consumers, and the different levels of service we'll provide. I'd show them what it would look like three years from now, then five years from now. And that was before one line of code had been written. You have to know your product, what the industry is all about, and what you are going to do.[5]

As one of the leaders we interviewed said to us, "I'm my organization's futures department." All leaders should view themselves this way. Because being forward-looking is the differentiating leadership credibility factor, you need to spend more time reading about, thinking about, and talking about the long-term view. Make it your business to spend time studying the future.

Set up a futures research committee to study potential changes and developments in areas affecting your organization. Put together a team to continually track fifty or sixty publications that represent new thoughts on trends in your domain. Ask them to prepare abstracts of articles they think have relevance. A smaller team can then pull the abstracts into reports for use in planning and decision making. Or simply have all the people in your organization regularly clip articles from newspapers, magazines, and websites. Circulate the ideas generated and discuss the impact of trends on your products, services, technologies, and constituents. Use these discussions to help you and your organization develop the ability to think long-term.

There are various ways you can classify and categorize the most significant business trends. The World Future Society recommends these six distinct categories: demographics, economics, government, environment, society, and technology to improve your understanding of the world around you.[6] Scanning what's going on today allows you to both look up from the short-term demands and look out toward the future so that you can begin to see how all the pieces of the puzzle fit together to form a picture of the future.

FORESIGHT: BE OPTIMISTIC

University of Southern California professor and leadership guru Warren Bennis suggests that "for leaders in today's and tomorrow's business climate" the appropriate motto is: "only the optimists survive." Warren writes that:

> Limits, constraints, and reduced expectations are the conventional prescriptions for our time. True

leaders, however, are able to see beyond an anemic
zeitgeist in order to sense opportunities that can
employ and house a multitude. Optimists have a
sixth sense for possibilities that realists can't or
won't see.[7]

Being optimistic doesn't mean failing to face up to
reality, hardship, and the struggles associated with getting extraordinary things accomplished. Indeed, the more
you understand reality the more prepared you can be to
act in ways that allow you to endure and even prosper in adversity. Medical researchers, for example, have
found that when confronted with a diagnosis of terminal
cancer some people live longer than others—and even
longer than expected. Norman Cousins, former editor of
Saturday Review and the author of more than twenty
books, who himself had to deal with a terminal disease,
studied those who beat the medical odds. He wrote
about his own experiences and his research into what
set apart the group of longer-term survivors, concluding
that "They responded with a fierce determination to
overcome. They didn't deny the diagnosis. They denied
the verdict that is usually associated with it."[8] The best
leaders are like that. They define the reality of our illness,
but defy the verdict that we are doomed.

Psychologist Martin Seligman has found a dramatic
difference between people who react to roadblocks with
a sense of futility—pessimists—and those who react

with a steely determination to master their destiny—optimists.[9] Those who learn to be optimistic about life are far more likely to be successful than those who view the current events through the lens of a pessimist. This means that your outlook on the future, and on life in general, strongly influences you and your group's success. In order to reach the top of that distant summit, you need to be optimistic, zestful, and energetic. You need to be curious about how things work and search for a deeper meaning and understanding of what's going on around you.

———

The Truth Is That Focusing On the Future Sets Leaders Apart. Your constituents expect you to know where you're going and to have a sense of direction. You have to be forward-looking; it's the quality that most differentiates leaders from individual contributors. Getting yourself and others focused on the exciting possibilities that the future holds is your special role on the team.

Developing the capacity to envision the future requires you to spend more time *in* the future—meaning more time reflecting on the future, more time reading about the future, and more time talking to others about the future. It's not an easy assignment, but it is an absolutely necessary one. It also requires you to reflect back on your past to discover the themes that really engage you and excite you. And it means thinking about the kind of legacy you want to leave and the contributions you want to make.

None of this can be done by a pessimist. You must remain optimistic and hopeful about what is yet to come. You must truly believe that the future will be brighter and be confident that we'll all get there together. A positive difference can only be made by a positive leader.

YOU CAN'T
DO IT ALONE

You might get the impression from what we've written so far that leadership is all about the leader. That'd be understandable, since we've talked about how leaders have to believe in themselves, how followers have to believe in their leaders, how leaders have to be clear about their values, and how leaders separate themselves from individual contributors with their visions of the future. All of this is true, but the reason it's true is because leaders are here to serve others, and not the other way around.

The Truth Is That You Can't Do It Alone. We learned this early in our research when Bill Flanagan, then manufacturing director for Amdahl Corporation, told us that he couldn't tell us about his personal best. We were quite surprised by his response, and we asked him why. Bill replied, "Because it wasn't my personal best. It was our personal best. It wasn't me, it was us." That was in 1984. In 2009 in Hong Kong, Eric Pan, regional head of the Chartered Institute of Management Accountants in South China, told us essentially the same thing when talking about his personal best leadership experience. "No matter how capable a leader is," Eric said, "he or she *alone* won't be able to deliver a large project or program without the joint efforts and synergies that come from the team."

Twenty-five years and half a world apart, Bill and Eric—and the thousands of other leaders who've told us their stories—remind us all that no leader single-handedly ever gets anything extraordinary done. We're absolutely certain that in another twenty-five years when someone asks a leader to share his or her personal best story, he or she will say exactly the same thing. Leadership is a team sport. There may be a captain, but without the team working together no one can score the winning goal.

Look at it this way. How do you know someone is a leader? While there are several hundred definitions of leadership in the academic literature, the simplest way to know is just to look to see whether that person has followers. If you think you're a leader and you turn around and no one is following you, then you're simply out for a walk.

YOU HAVE TO MAKE A HUMAN CONNECTION

Leadership is not about the leader *per se*. It is not about you alone. It's about the relationship between leaders and their constituents. It's about the connection you and your teammates have with each other. It's about how you behave and feel toward each other. It's about the emotional bond that exists between you and them. Exemplary leaders know that they must attend to the needs, and focus on the capabilities, of their constituents if they are going to get extraordinary things done.

The Center for Creative Leadership found that the critical success factor for the top three jobs in organizations is "relationships with subordinates."[1] Similar studies on leadership and emotional intelligence done by Daniel Goleman and others validate this finding.[2] Human connection is a fact of life. Claudio Fernandez-Araoz, a former partner and now senior advisor in the executive search firm of Egon Zehnder International, has personally conducted several hundred senior executive search projects, and as the former director of Egon Zehnder International's professional development for their fifty-eight offices worldwide, he was exposed to several thousand hiring cases. He told us that all this evidence . . .

... clearly demonstrated that the classic profile organizations look for in hiring a senior executive (relevant experience and outstanding IQ) is much more a predictor of failure than success, unless the relevant emotional intelligence competencies are also present. In fact, serious weaknesses in the domain of emotional intelligence predict failure at senior levels with amazing accuracy.[3]

This is serious stuff. You can graduate at the top of the class from the best business schools in the world; reason circles around your brightest peers; solve technical problems with wizard-like powers; have the relevant situational, functional, and industry experience; and *still* be more likely to fail than succeed—unless you also possess the requisite personal and social skills. The mandate is very clear. Build your own and your team members' abilities to work with each other. Doing this well will have a direct impact on your personal and organizational success.

YOU HAVE TO HEAR WHAT PEOPLE ARE SAYING

So often leadership is associated with inspirational speaking, but people often miss the fact that making the human connection requires exceptional listening. You have to understand the perspective of others, and that ability has been shown to be the most glaring difference between successful and unsuccessful leaders.[4]

Sensitivity to others' needs is a truly precious human ability. But it is not a complex act. It simply means spending time with people on the factory floor or in the showroom or warehouse or back room. It means being acutely aware of the attitudes and feelings of others and the nuances of their communication.

It's about intimacy. It's about familiarity. It's about empathy. This kind of communication requires understanding constituents at a much deeper level than most people normally find comfortable. It requires understanding others' strongest yearnings and their deepest fears. It requires a profound awareness of their joys and their sorrows. It requires experiencing life as they experience it.

When you listen, when you hear, and when you truly understand the needs of your constituents, you will connect with them in ways that an out-of-touch leader cannot. You will make a primal connection. "The leader acts as the group's emotional guide," write Daniel Goleman, Richard Boyatzis, and Annie McKee in *Primal Leadership*. They go on to say that the primordial task of leadership is "driving the collective emotions in a positive direction and clearing the emotional smog created by toxic emotions."[5]

When leaders are in tune with the emotions of others, they create *resonance* between leader and constituent and among constituents, much like the musicians in an orchestra create resonance when their instruments are in tune.[6] Insensitive, tone-deaf leaders drive negative emotions and create dissonance in a group. This discord is highly destructive to the group's functioning. Only resonant leaders generate the amplification that enables groups to produce exceptional results.

UNITE PEOPLE AROUND A SHARED VISION

One of the most powerful internal motivators on the planet is a sense of meaning and purpose.[7] Throughout human history people have risked life, security, and wealth for something that is greater than themselves. People want a chance to take part in something meaningful and important. There is a deep human yearning to make a difference. People want to know that there is a purpose to their existence. They want to know that their lives mean something. A significant part of the leader's job is uncovering and reflecting back the meaning that others seek.

Leadership is very much a two-way street. As Elaine Fan, food scientist at National Starch Food Innovation, explains:

> You must understand the needs of your followers. I have never encountered a circumstance in

which leadership was a one-way street. You won't
be a leader for very long if you only do what you
want to do. In all of my group meetings, no one
has ever been successful in just ordering others
around to achieve only one person's goals. The
most efficient and successful groups that I have
been a part of have been when one person takes
the lead while asking everyone else their opinions. The leader merely coordinates and puts into
action the wants and desires of the group. A leader
must know and understand the needs of the rest
of the group or soon he/she won't be leading
anyone.

When listening with sensitivity to the aspirations of
others, as Elaine advises, you can discover the common
values that link people together. And by knowing those
aspirations, you are able to stand before others and
say with assurance: "Here is what I heard you say that
you want for yourselves. Here is how your own needs
and interests will be served by enlisting in a common
purpose."

You have to know your constituents, and you have
to speak to them in language they will find engaging. If
you're trying to mobilize people to move in a particular
direction, then you've got to talk about that future des-
tination in ways that others find appealing to them. It's
got to be something that *they* care about as much as, or
even more than, you do.

Truly inspirational leadership is not about selling a vision; it's about showing people how the vision can directly benefit them and how their specific needs can be satisfied. Leaders must be able to sense the purpose in others. What people really want to hear is not the leader's vision. They want to hear about how their own aspirations will be met. They want to hear how their dreams will come true and their hopes will be realized. They want to see themselves in the picture of the future that the leader is painting. The very best leaders understand that it's about inspiring a *shared* vision, not about selling their own idiosyncratic views of the world.

The vast majority of people want to walk with their leaders. They want to dream with them. They want to invent with them. They want to be involved in creating their own futures. This means that you have to stop taking the view that visions come from the top down. You have to stop seeing it as a monologue, and you have to start engaging others in a collective dialogue about the future.[8]

MAKE OTHERS FEEL STRONG AND CAPABLE

Because extraordinary achievements don't result simply from the actions of the leader, it is critical that you build a team of people who feel powerful and capable of taking action. That's precisely what we find in our research when we ask people to describe their relationships with the leader they most admire and look up to. They tell us that when they are with this leader they feel empowered, listened to, understood, capable, important, like they mattered, challenged to do more, and other similar descriptors. The overwhelming sense we get from reviewing thousands and thousands of these responses is that the best leaders take actions that make people strong and capable. They make people feel that they can do more than they thought they could. One of the reasons people want to follow a leader is because they know that they will be better off as a result of being in that relationship than they would be otherwise.

There's a famous restaurant scene in the Academy Award-winning film *As Good As It Gets*, where Carol (portrayed by actress Helen Hunt) becomes so exasperated with Melvin (portrayed by actor Jack Nicholson) that she finally gets up from the table and is ready to leave. Melvin looks at her quite stunned. He has no idea that he's just insulted her. He asks her to sit down, and she responds, "Melvin, pay me a compliment. I need one and quick. You have no idea how much what you said just hurt my feelings."

Melvin is put on the spot. He mutters something and Carol tells him that it's not a compliment. She demands, "Now or never." Melvin pauses for a moment, and then

says to Carol: "You make me want to be a better man."
Carol is so astonished by this remark that she exclaims:
"I think this is about the best compliment of my life."[9]

Now think about what Melvin was really saying: "As a
result of this relationship I'm a better person. And I want
to be in this relationship with you because being in this
relationship makes me better off than I would be on my
own." Put this into an organizational context, and think
about how important it is to know that your manager
believes in you, supports you, and will back you up. The
same goes for your constituents. They want to know that
you'll make them better off than they are.

In fact, that's what Jerry Zhang, associate director,
auto business, Guangdong Yi Hang Enterprise Development, told us about strengthening others:

> We cannot just throw the work to people without
> helping them to do it. We must know the person.
> We must give him confidence. We must let him
> know what he will learn from the work, and that
> this will make him feel more competent and better
> able to achieve a more difficult task.
>
> For example, there was a financial manager
> in my company. When he first joined the com-
> pany he was assigned to do the budget for next
> year. He absolutely was good at budgeting, but he
> did not know very well the industry which he had
> just entered. I spent a lot of time sharing industry
> information and operating processes with him.

> Together we also went out and visited the mar-
> ket many times to help him know more about the
> industry. As a result the work was well done.

Getting people to feel capable and confident, and to act like leaders themselves, requires making an investment in their personal development, which is what Sharon Miao, project engineer at Lexmark International, reported. She told us about how she helped one of the engineers on her team get promoted. She described him as very experienced, with good technical knowledge and skills, but that his oral English was not very good. Based on her observations she felt that, while his English knowledge level was good enough, he wasn't very confident about speaking in English. He was "too shy," she said. She took a series of deliberate actions to help him develop his confidence and skills speaking in English. When he was subsequently promoted, the new manager told Sharon that "he would have been promoted much sooner if his oral English ability was as good as it was now."

From this experience Sharon learned how important it is to truly believe that your direct reports can be better, and that, as a leader, you need to convince them of their potential. Often, people just lack a little courage and confidence. They blossom when they have a leader who believes in them and gives them support and encouragement.

BRING IT OUT OF OTHERS

John Hamm, entrepreneur, CEO, venture capitalist, and leadership educator at Santa Clara University, explains that many leaders fall into the trap of thinking that it's their responsibility to be the one who has all the answers. This puts you into, he says:

> ... a very lonely, isolated position where information becomes unreliable and useful input is stifled. Effective leaders, by contrast, understand that their role is to bring out the answers in others. They do this by very clearly and explicitly seeking contributions, challenges, and collaboration from the people who report to them, using their positional power not to dominate but rather to drive the decision-making process.[10]

Rather than thinking that you have all the answers, you need to be able to ask great questions. Great questions send people on pioneering journeys in their minds. They're a lot more likely to discover novel ideas when you set them free to explore on their own. The answers are out there, and they will be found among your constituents as long as people feel safe in offering them. Ask your colleagues to read about your industry and field, especially stories about what other innovative companies are doing, and ask why this isn't being done in your organization. What are they hearing from their colleagues who do business in this area? What are the next things that should be focused on? What are the stumbling blocks ahead?

Asking questions is just one way that you can communicate that you believe in other people's abilities. Giving them choices, providing them with discretion over how things are done, and fostering accountability are others. People want to feel in charge of their own lives. They want to be in control. They want to determine their own destinies. They want to know that their input matters, that their ideas are good ones, that their answers are correct, and that their decisions will be supported. It's your job as a leader to increase people's sense of self-determination, self-confidence, and personal effectiveness.

High-quality relationships don't happen spontaneously. They require leadership. It's your job to interact with others in ways that promote connection, collaboration, confidence, and competence. When you do, you'll see learning, innovation, and performance soar.

————

The Truth Is That You Can't Do It Alone. Leaders alone don't make anything great. Leadership is a shared responsibility. You need others, and they need you.

You're all in this together. To build and sustain that sense of oneness, exemplary leaders are sensitive to the needs of others. They ask questions. They listen. They provide support. They develop skills. They ask for help. They align people in a common cause. They make people feel like anything is possible. They connect people to their need to be in charge of their own lives. They enable others to be even better than they already are.

TRUST RULES

In a 2009 international study, the majority of people said they trust a stranger more than they trust their boss.[1]

Think about what this finding means if you're a manager. It means that there's a good chance that the people you lead are less likely to trust you than to trust someone they simply walked by on the way to work.

Think about what this means to your credibility. Credibility is the foundation of leadership, we've said, and trustworthiness is an essential component of credibility. This means that if people don't trust you, they won't believe what you say.

Think about what it means to the organization's performance. High-trust organizations have been shown to outperform low-trust organizations by 286 percent in total return to shareholders. A PricewaterhouseCoopers study of corporate innovation among the *Financial Times* 100 showed that the number one differentiating factor between the top innovators and the bottom innovators was trust.[2] That means that if people don't trust you, your organization is likely to under-perform and be slow to innovate.

That's why for Jill Cleveland the first order of business when she became finance manager at Apple was "to learn to trust my employees. After being responsible only for me for so long, it was very difficult to have to relinquish control. But I understood that in order for my employees, and thus myself, to be successful, I needed to develop a cohesive and collaborative team, beginning with trust as the framework." If you are going to have the same success that Jill and the others leaders we've studied have had, and if you're going to build cohesive teams, then you, too, must create a structure for trust in your organization. Without it you can't lead.

The Truth Is That Trust Rules. Trust rules your personal credibility. Trust rules your ability to get things done. Trust rules your team's cohesiveness. Trust rules your organization's innovativeness and performance. Trust rules your brand image. Trust rules just about everything you do.

INCREASE YOUR TRUST, INCREASE YOUR INFLUENCE

Researchers have found that the level of trust that constituents have in their leaders determines the amount of influence they will willingly accept. In an experiment on the impact of trust on group problem solving, leaders in a high-trust condition had greater influence on group members and were more willing to accept influence attempts by group members than were leaders in a low-trust condition. This same study also found that high trust led to greater acceptance of group member interdependence, more cooperation, and enhanced information flow among all group members.[3] Studies involving soldiers in combat in Iraq found that the more the soldiers trusted their platoon leaders, the more willing they were to accept their leader's influence concerning their motivation to become better group members, strive for excellence, and improve as a person.[4] Even in a traditional command-and-control environment, trust comes first and following comes second, not the other way around. Trust motivates people to go beyond mere compliance with authority. It motivates them to reach for the best in themselves, their team, and their organization. There's a very powerful message here, and all leaders need to pay attention to it.

In another field study investigating how new company presidents establish working relationships with key subordinates, the level of influence both leaders and constituents could exercise was a function of the amount of trust that existed between the two parties.[5] Florian Bennhold gave us an example from his personal experience that underscores this point. When he was being recruited, he described how Wilson Rickerson, president at Rickerson Energy Strategies, from their first meeting . . .

> . . . built our relationship on trust and he made
> clear that he was willing to take the first step.
> I was excited to work with him because I felt
> that he trusted my abilities. Not only did I feel
> compelled to reciprocate his trust, but I also felt
> empowered to explore new avenues.

Tremendous energy is unleashed when constituents trust you. Like Florian, they feel liberated, self-confident, and secure enough in their relationships to explore new territories and opportunities, and take on fresh challenges. People won't take risks unless they feel safe. They need to feel secure that they will not be unfairly treated, embarrassed, harassed, harmed, or hurt when taking action.

There's a positive relationship between risk and trust. The more people trust, the more they'll risk. When people feel secure, because they trust that you and the organization will protect their welfare, they can focus their energies on meeting higher-order needs, such as forming strong and cohesive relationships, mastering tasks, achieving organizational objectives, gaining a greater sense of self-efficacy, learning new skills and knowledge necessary to prepare for future assignments, and pursuing activities that promote growth and develop innate potential.

YOU HAVE TO ANTE UP FIRST

Trust is the framework that supports all relationships. Building that structure of trust begins when one person takes a risk and opens up to another. If you're the leader in the relationship, that person needs to be you. You need to ante up first.

That can be a scary proposition. When you trust, you're taking a chance. You're betting that others will keep you safe, that they'll take good care of the information you communicate, the resources you allocate, and the feelings you share. You're taking the risk that the other party won't take advantage of you or harm you, physically or psychologically. You're relying on them to do what's right. You're counting on them to do their part. Your influence is at stake, your money may be at risk, and your dreams are on the line. And, especially in the beginning, there's absolutely no guarantee that if you trust first the other party will reciprocate.

Even so, you have to be the first to trust. You have to go first because people who demonstrate trust in others are seen as more trustworthy themselves. And vice versa: People who do not trust others are perceived as not being worthy of other people's trust. It's that all-too-common lament: "If he doesn't trust me, why should I trust him?" Someone has to start the positive cycle of trust, and it's rightfully the leader's job.

Dawn Lindblom, for example, wanted to know whether she could trust Gail McGovern, the new president and CEO of the national Red Cross. Dawn, who only recently had been appointed the executive director for the Red Cross in Eastern Washington, had the chance to find out. Gail was touring the nation and introducing herself to the organization's regional leaders and this trust question was put to her point-blank in one of those meeting: "Can we trust you?" Gail's response was: "I can't answer that for you, but let me tell you that I trust each and every one of you." Dawn told us that it made all the difference in the world to her knowing that Gail was going first, that Gail would earn their trust by taking the first step and trusting them, their commitment, and their competence.

This same willingness to go first when it comes to trust also matters at an organizational level. USAA provides insurance, investment, and banking services to over 5.5 million members around the world, employs nearly 22,000 people, and has owned and managed assets exceeding $96 billion. Their focus on customer service is consistent from the top of the organization all the way down to first line employees. As Vic Andrews, the recently retired vice president and general manager of USAA's Mountain States Regional Office, describes: "We believe our members. A real simple example of this is when a member calls us and says, 'my child is sixteen years old and is a high school honors student.' That results in a discount. We say 'fine, thank you very much,' and we give the discount. We don't require the member to send in the student's report card; we don't ask for a letter from his or her principal, we just believe because, as a USAA member, until you prove otherwise, we believe what you say. It's about trust. We trust the members and they trust us."[6] It's this kind of trusting relationship with customers that earned the company in 2009, for the third consecutive year, one of the top two spots as *BusinessWeek*'s "Customer Service Champs."[7] High levels of trust pay off in the marketplace as well as inside the organization.

YOU HAVE TO SHOW THAT YOU CAN BE TRUSTED

Trust may seem quite intangible at times, but it's earned in some very tangible ways. You have to demonstrate to others that you have both the character (honesty and integrity) and the abilities (competence and expertise) to do your job and to look out for their welfare.

We got a very real sense of this at a recent management development program involving outdoor initiatives. As a trust-building exercise, the participants went abseiling—a controlled descent down a rope, sometimes called rappelling. Talk about needing to trust before you risk! Here we were descending into a dark cave with only a rope and harness to hold us. It was scary. To gain our trust—our belief that we'd be safe in taking the risk—the team leader outfitted the heftiest member of the group with the belay equipment, then lifted him up and left him dangling four or five feet off the ground. While he was suspended there, the team leader proceeded to tell us about the characteristics of the safety system—the harness, webbing, and rope. Then she took a knife and systematically cut the fibers of the rope holding our compatriot until only one strand remained. To our amazement and relief, one strand was still enough to hold him. After this demonstration, we were ready to put our trust in both her and the system and face up to the challenges of vertically descending into the cave. There was no doubt in our minds that we could believe what she told and showed us.

Analogously, you need to demonstrate that you have the competence, the system, and the processes to make people feel safe and trusting. You have to do it in real time by dealing with situations that might create fear and suspicion. You have to extend yourself by being available, by volunteering information, by sharing your personal experiences, and by making connections with the experiences and aspirations of your constituents.

Gigi Xie, territory manager for seventeen retail gas stations for BP Petrochina Petroleum in Southern China, faced just such a situation. She told us about a customer service campaign her company launched and how she needed to rely on all of her team members to meet the initiative. She began by sending them all an email that explained "we're all in the same boat" and how everyone would need to be involved to meet this challenge. "Let's try our best together," she said.

The results from the first month of the service campaign were good, but in the second month performance declined. Gigi said that it was time to "show trust to build trust." She attended all-hands meetings in the poor customer service sites and told them that she "wouldn't punish anyone because we trust that you can improve." She said that because people knew that this decision (not to punish people for poor performance) put her at some risk with her management, "they were touched and promised to change." All of these poor-performing sites did, in fact, improve their performance considerably in the succeeding months. Gigi felt that the key to success in this critical incident was the customer service representatives' confidence that she trusted them, even when they were having difficulties: "I believe that a solid trust platform is needed if we are to get a united, cooperative team to head in the same direction.''

Trusting others encourages them to trust you. Distrusting others persuades them to distrust you. As Gigi learned, the leader has to build a "solid platform of trust" in order to generate superior performance.

It's in your best interest to be trusted. When other people trust you, your actions will generate fewer ambiguities and disputes. How can you facilitate trust? Research has shown that a few key behaviors contribute to whether or not others perceive you as trustworthy.[8] Here are four actions to keep in mind:

• **Behave predictably and consistently.** When you are reliable and others know they can count on you, then your words and actions will have greater power to influence them. If your behavior is confusing, indecisive, or inconsistent, then others cannot depend upon you to behave in certain ways across similar situations or make reasonable hypotheses about how you might react under new or different circumstances. Some degree of successful predictability is required in order for people to believe and trust in you. Predictability is also about consistency. Consistency means that the same personal values and organizational aims will influence what you say and do.

• **Communicate clearly.** When you make statements about your intentions—however tentative they may be in your own mind—you need to be aware that to others these same statements are viewed as promises. If you frequently make statements that you don't intend as commitments, but that others might reasonably interpret as such, then they will have reason to believe that you are unreliable and not trustworthy. When you are clear about what you mean, then there is less chance that others will find your statements misleading.

- **Treat promises seriously.** The more seriously you treat your own commitments, the more seriously others will treat them. The same dynamic is true when you make promises lightly. If you don't take them seriously, then others won't either. Problems arise when people have different perceptions of the importance of both your word and the circumstances required to justify *not* keeping your promise. Further complications occur when people can't distinguish between wishes or vague promises on your part and those to which you're seriously committed.

- **Be forthright and candid.** When you are forthright and don't deceive others, they will have less reason to be angry or deceive you in return. They will be less suspicious and better able to deal with legitimate differences. There is no such thing as a little bit of dishonesty. Discovering that someone has been dishonest casts doubt over everything he says and does. By the way, honesty doesn't require full disclosure. It does, however, require a clear indication of areas about which full disclosure should not be expected and an explanation of why it's not appropriate. Still, greater disclosure between people generally makes for better working relationships and easier resolution of problems should they arise.

Mark Twain once said, "If you tell the truth, you don't have to remember anything." The failure to heed his advice is precisely what gives rise to public distrust, and to the popularity of the cartoon strip *Dilbert*, in which nearly every day another cynical joke is played off common distrust and disconnections between a pretentious and autocratic boss and often clueless direct reports. Generating greater trust between people is the only way to overcome the frustration, disillusionment, and suspicion that so often plagues groups, organizations, and societies. Trust is the best antidote to cynicism, and the most potent anti-Dilbert vaccine around.

COMMUNICATE WITH A NEED-TO-SHARE MENTALITY

In their book *Building the High Trust Organization*, Pam Shockley-Zalabak, Sherry Morreale, and Michael Hackman describe the need to replace the traditional "need to know" mentality of communications with a "need to share" approach. They explain:

> A "need to know" approach tightly controls information while a "need to share" mentality fosters information exchange important for trust. A "need to know" approach (although sometimes necessary) signals distrust by limiting access to information. A "need to share" approach signals trust by providing access and response to information whether receivers have an immediate "need" for the information or not. The "need to share" approach provides information employees need in a timely and useful manner. A "need to share" approach stimulates employees at all organizational levels to communicate information critical for problem solving, change, and innovation.[9]

Your job as a leader is to make sure that people get the information they want and need, when they want and need it, and in a form they can use and understand. Building trust goes way beyond telling the truth. You have to communicate on a timely basis and in a readily accessible and easily understood manner. When information is not forthcoming, is late, or is perceived to have been withheld, distrust begins to build. When full information is not forthcoming, interpretations generated almost always become more negative and cynical than they would have been had the truth been presented up front.

When there is an information vacuum, people will make up their own answers. And these answers are more likely to be negative and cynical than to be the truth. Waiting to disseminate information is often justified as a desire to gather more certain and complete information, but waiting often contributes to distrust. "I wonder what they are not telling me?" you may ask yourself. Or you say, "I wonder why they are not telling me about it? They must have something to hide."

CHA, a U.K.-based consultancy, found that 90 percent of employees who are kept fully informed are motivated to deliver added value by staying with a company longer and working harder, while 80 percent of those who are kept in the dark are not. In addition, they reported that organizations with effective communication are 4.5 times more likely to report high levels of employee engagement, and companies with high levels of communication effectiveness are 20 percent more likely to report lower turnover rates than their competitors.[10]

When it comes to sustaining trust over the long term, you have to communicate, communicate, and communicate. Selectively sharing information, failing to keep people informed, and telling people too late about matters important to their work only leads to distrust and suspicion. It's also important to be clear, timely, and relevant. There's a lot of noise and static in this media-rich world. You have to be able to get information to the eyes and ears of those who need it when they need it. Openness is one of the major drivers of trust, and sharing information is one of the major ways that you express your openness with others and signal your trust in them.

———

The Truth Is That Trust Rules. Getting people to work together begins with building mutual trust. Before asking for trust from others, you must demonstrate your own trust in them. That means taking the risk of disclosing what you stand for, value, want, hope for, and are willing and unwilling to do. You also have to be predictable and consistent in your actions; forthright, candid, and clear in your communication; and serious about your promises. And, as we've learned so many times, leaders are far better served when they're forthcoming with information. There's nothing more destructive to trust than deceit, and nothing more constructive than candor.

CHALLENGE IS THE CRUCIBLE FOR GREATNESS

Leaders are no strangers to challenges—all you have to do is reflect on leaders throughout history. Think about historical leaders you personally admire—leaders you'd be willing to follow if they were alive today. We've been asking people to do this simple exercise for three decades, and the result is always the same: The historical leaders whom people admire most always faced and led others through major challenges.

When people think of the business leaders they admire, they think about people who have turned around failing companies, started entrepreneurial ventures, developed breakthrough products and services, or transformed industries. When they talk about community, government, military, or non-governmental leaders, they discuss men and women who liberated people from tyranny, fought for human rights, won wars, struggled against oppression, organized movements for change, or suffered greatly for their causes. Challenge was the context in which these leaders operated, and change was the theme of all their campaigns.

You don't have to study historical leaders to learn this lesson. You can just look at everyday leaders such as yourself and those down the hall or across the street. When we first analyzed the initial set of personal best leadership cases nearly three decades ago, what immediately struck us was that people always chose situations in which they were challenged in very significant ways. It's the same story today. For example, here is what Katherine Winkel, marketing communications coordinator at Monsanto, had to say about a discussion in one of our seminars about her peers' personal best leadership experiences.

> The similarity that most stuck out in my mind at the time, and indeed remains with me, was that in each story the person described having to overcome uncertainty and fear in order to achieve his or her best. Whatever the case, staring down uncertainty and ultimately overcoming this hurdle was a major theme.
>
> Typically, you would think people would describe uncertainty and fear as negative or even

demotivating factors in leadership, but here it
seems they are almost prerequisites for success! It
has taught me that uncertainty is a necessity that
drives us to do our very best.

The personal best leadership cases, as Katherine
observed, are about triumphs over adversity, departures
from the past, about doing things that had never been
done before, about going to places not yet discovered.
They are all about challenge and change.

What's significant about this finding is that we didn't
ask people to tell us about challenge or change. We
asked them to tell us about personal best leadership
experiences. They could have discussed any leadership experience, but they chose to talk about times when
they were tested. Not one single person claimed to have
achieved a personal best by keeping things the same.

**The Truth Is That Challenge Is the Crucible for
Greatness.** The study of leadership is the study of how
men and women guide people through uncertainty, hardship, disruption, transformation, transition, recovery,
new beginnings, and other significant challenges. It's also
the study of how men and women, in times of constancy
and complacency, actively seek to disturb the status quo,
awaken new possibilities, and pursue opportunities.

As the late John Gardner, advisor to four U.S. presidents and founder of Common Cause, was fond of

saying: "What we have before us are some breathtaking opportunities disguised as insoluble problems."[1] Sometimes leaders have to shake things up. Other times they just have to grab hold of the adversity that surrounds them. Whether challenge comes from the outside or the inside, leaders make things happen. Leadership and challenge are simply inseparable.

BRICK WALLS TEST COMMITMENT

Challenge, hardship, risk, and adversity aren't hard to find. Just take a look around today's neighborhoods, homes, and workplaces, and you'll see lots of things that aren't going as well as they could. There are no shortages of opportunities to change the way things are. The personal bests that people have shared are clear examples of how important it is to view challenge as an opportunity and not as a threat.

Challenges cause you to come face-to-face with yourself. They are rather harsh ways of reminding you of what's important, what you value, and where you want to go. Many people have experienced life-threatening, even torturous circumstances, and have found ways to turn them into tests of strength and determination. One such experience is the story of computer science professor Randy Pausch, who delivered his now-famous "last lecture" at Carnegie Mellon University, a one-of-a-kind speech that made the world stop and pay attention.[2] In his talk, Randy, who was dying of pancreatic cancer at the time, said, "The brick walls are there for a reason. They're not there to keep us out. The brick walls are there to give us a chance to show how badly we want something."[3]

Randy's personal circumstances at the time were certainly unique to him, but his observation is applicable to everyone. It's especially relevant to leaders. The challenges today are not any more insurmountable than the ones faced by so many others. Several generations have now successfully dealt with world wars, economic depressions, and natural disasters. Similarly, each generation has had to, and will continue to have to, adapt to technological innovations, scientific advancements, and cultural shifts. What might seem like brick walls are simply doors to a new future, asking: "What do you want? And how badly do you want it?"

Sometimes those brick walls are external to the organization. Sometimes they are internal. Most often they aren't a matter of life and death, as Randy Pausch experienced, nor are they as huge and dramatic as those challenges that make news headlines. Usually, they are barriers that you encounter every day on the job—a reluctant team, an over-controlling boss, or a boring routine. Whether the challenge is large or small, leaders take charge of change.

"Everyone can make a difference if she or he dares to step out to seize the opportunity and take the initiative," declared Sam Liu, a front-line manager responsible for shuttle truck operation management between Hong Kong and Shenzhen, China. This operation had been going for six years, there were three shifts per day, and "we were pretty busy, and sometimes we made some mistakes because there were so many shipping orders flooding in." Still, Sam found that "frankly speaking, the job was boring. I thought that I could not spend my time on this simple and boring job. I wanted to make some changes in order to not only free myself from this job but also improve the whole process." After getting approval from his manager, he worked with his counterparts to develop a new truck order processing system that is still in place today. What was the take-away lesson for Sam? Here's what he told us:

> The impact of this change was big for both management and for me. To management, they did not expect this kind of change would be raised from the front-line staff, and they did not even realize the urgency for change on such a low-level operational procedure. After they witnessed the effect of the change, they became more amenable to our attempt to change. To me, I realized the importance of observation and looking around. Even in a very normal and simple job, we can find

some opportunities to change or improve if we observe carefully. And if we dare to challenge the procedure by taking some calculated risk, we will have a good chance to influence others and lead the change successfully.

Whether on the front lines or in the executive suites, whether at the global or local levels, leaders see open doors while others see brick walls. Leaders seize the opportunities that hide inside adversities. They take the initiative to move things forward.

STRENGTHEN RESILIENCE

As Sam Liu can tell you, confronting challenges and making changes can be stressful. And too much stress can threaten the immune system and make us sick. That's why successfully leading change requires resilience.[4] In order to learn how to thrive under adverse circumstances and recover from setbacks, you first need to embrace the challenge. Change always opens up all kinds of new and exciting possibilities for the future. What are these for you? What are some innovative solutions that you can explore? How can you go about searching for new and innovative solutions that might lead you and your colleagues (organization) out of your current situation?

In addition, you need to be able to control what you can. You obviously don't control all of what is happening in the broader environment, but you are still in charge of your own life. What decisions and actions do you and others control? How can you, and others, positively influence the outcome? What factors *are* in your control, and how can you all stay focused on them? Furthermore, while you may not control what is happening in the larger environment, you can control how you respond to the news about what you are facing. You need to believe that you can beneficially influence the direction and outcome of what is going on around you through your own efforts.

Be willing to take charge of change. People who are proactive are more engaged in the practices of exemplary leaders than those who are reactive, and, no surprise, they find themselves feeling more successful as well as healthier.[5] Leaders with high hope are not Pollyannas. They acknowledge reality, but they also move quickly to mobilize personal and group resources to deal with problems.

To be a leader you need to make something happen. You need to feel a strong sense of commitment, believing that you can find something in whatever you are doing that is interesting, important, or worthwhile. Consider taking actions that create forward momentum, even little things that can get you moving in the right direction.

The good news is that you can learn how to respond constructively to adversity and change. Resilience is not a trait that you either have or don't have; it's not something that's genetically determined. These behaviors, thoughts, and actions can be learned and developed.

GET GRITTY

It takes determination and strength to deal with the adversities of life and leadership. You can't let the setbacks get you down or the roadblocks get in your way. You can't become overly discouraged when things don't go according to plan. You can't give up when the resistance builds or when the competition gets stiff. Neither can you let other tempting new projects divert your attention. You can't lose focus when there are lots of distractions all around. You can't hop from one thing to the next without completing what you started. You have to stay focused on your dream. You have to stick with it. You have to overcome. You must never give up. That is what leaders do when they're at their personal best. It's what you must do to achieve yours.

It's called grit. Grit is that firmness of spirit, that unyielding courage that is essential in dealing with challenge. And researchers are finding that it plays an essential role in attaining difficult goals. Angela Duckworth, professor of psychology at the University of Pennsylvania, and her colleagues define grit very simply as "perseverance and passion for long-term goals" and report that it "entails working strenuously toward challenges, maintaining effort and interest over years despite failure, adversity, and plateaus in progress."[6] They've developed a test to measure it, asking about such things as setting goals, being obsessed with an idea or project, maintaining focus, sticking with things that take a long time to complete, overcoming setbacks, and the like. They've studied the grit of kids in school, cadets in the military, working professionals, artists, academics, and others. Their results convincingly demonstrate that people with more grit are more likely to achieve positive outcomes. Angela makes this summary comment about the findings of her work: "I'll bet that there isn't a single successful person who hasn't depended on grit. Nobody is talented enough to not have to work hard, and that's what grit allows you to do."[7]

Consider the results from these two interesting studies. The first involved finalists in the 2005 Scripps National Spelling Bee (participants included thousands of children from the United States, Europe, Canada, New Zealand, Guam, Jamaica, Puerto Rico, the U.S. Virgin Islands, the Bahamas, and American Samoa). Gritty finalists—that is, those who scored high on passion and perseverance—worked harder and longer than their less gritty peers and, as a consequence, performed better. (And keep in mind that this sample was already biased toward the "best of the best" finalists).[8]

The second study involved, again, the "best of the best" in a very challenging environment: First-year cadets at the United States Military Academy (West Point). Grit predicted completion of their rigorous summer training program—referred to as "Beast Barracks"—better than any other variable, including high school rank, SAT score, leadership potential score, or physical aptitude.[9]

This means that you need to find a goal that can sustain your interest and the interest of those around you for some considerable time. To be the most successful, you and your constituents must have a passion for a purpose and the perseverance to hang with it for the long term. This focus gives meaning to sticking through the hard times and to dealing with the often-inevitable disappointments and setbacks that accompany any significant accomplishment.

In reflecting back on the challenging experiences that people wrote about in their personal bests—and the challenging experiences that characterized the admired historical leaders—it is very clear that grit played a role. Leaders and constituents alike felt passionately committed to a cause, and they were willing to suffer through the tough times that came with doing something difficult and demanding.

Finally, engage in some positive self-talk. Acknowledge the challenges and difficulties, but then tell yourself, and others, that these challenges can be overcome with hard work and determination. When you have true grit, you learn from your setbacks and are always willing to keep trying.

FAILING IS LEARNING

Whenever you're challenging the status quo, whenever you're tackling demanding problems, whenever you're making meaningful changes, whenever you're confronting adversity, you will sometimes fail. Despite how much you see challenge as an opportunity, despite how focused you can be, despite how driven you are to succeed, there will, no doubt, be setbacks. Think again about leaders throughout history who are remembered for their greatness. Some lost battles, some were imprisoned, some saw their businesses shut down, and most were ridiculed while trying to achieve the extraordinary. Mistakes happen. Defeats occur. Failure is inevitable. None of these are dirty words to leaders. Rather, they are signs that you're doing something tough, exacting, and out-of-the-ordinary. That's why you need grit. It's also why you need to see failure as learning.

A friend of ours once told us a story about his first day of skiing classes. He skied all day long, he recalled, and he didn't fall down once. He was absolutely elated. He skied up to the ski instructor and told him about the great day that he'd had. His ski instructor was not impressed in the least. The instructor said, "Personally, I think you had a lousy day." Our friend was stunned by the feedback. "What do you mean I had a lousy day?" he asked rather defensively. "Isn't the objective to stay up on these skis and not to fall down?" The ski instructor looked him straight in the eye and replied, "If you're not falling, you're not learning."

That ski instructor understood that if you can stand up on your skis all day long the first time out, you're doing only what's comfortable, not pushing yourself to try anything new or difficult. When you try to do something you don't know how to do, you'll fall down. That's guaranteed.

The point isn't to promote falling down or failing for its own sake. The point is that, when you're experimenting with new ideas and trying out new methods and techniques, you have to accept failure as part of the process. And when mistakes and failures happen, you have to ask, "What can be learned from this experience?" Learning doesn't take place in the absence of mistakes.

This is precisely what Mark Linsky, former Hewlett-Packard manager, now on the national board of AYSO (American Youth Soccer Organization), told us about one of the central lessons of his career. "Leaders improve because they make mistakes." He explained that "They view feedback as a gift that helps them to learn how to get even better the next time around. For leaders, learning needs to be a continual process." Mark reminds us that, while a lot can be learned from success, it's often your failures and your mistakes that are your best teachers—if, of course, you are willing to accept the feedback, figure out what you can do better, and put that learning into practice the next time around.

———

The Truth Is That Challenge Is the Crucible for Greatness. All significant and meaningful accomplishments involve adversity, difficulty, change, and challenge. No one ever got anything extraordinary done by keeping things the same. Risk, uncertainty, and hardships test us. Initiative and grit are imperatives in times of uncertainty. You have to embrace the challenge, control what you can, and take charge of change to be successful in these turbulent times. To deal with setbacks and to bounce back from mistakes, you need grit. You also need to find ways to learn from failure, knowing that it's one of the best teachers you can have.

YOU EITHER LEAD BY EXAMPLE OR YOU DON'T LEAD AT ALL

Jazz virtuoso Dizzy Gillespie once said, "That trumpet is lying in the case every day, waiting for me."[1] In the same sense, leadership is waiting for you every day. It's waiting for you to take action. It's waiting for you to show others that you mean what you say. It's waiting for you to demonstrate that you know how to get people moving. In the final analysis, leadership is about playing that instrument called "you." But when you perform, you have to make sure that you play in tune. Your audience won't applaud dissonant notes.

That was certainly the insight that Casey Mork, manager of the new product team, shared with us about one of his first supervisors, someone Casey felt wasn't clear about his values, never "had a true voice," and said one thing and did another. "As could be predicted," explained Casey, "With the lack of a model at the top, our group failed in internal cohesion, customer experience, and business results." Casey learned what every aspiring leader must realize:

> You've got to walk the talk, not just talk the talk.
> Leaders are responsible for modeling behavior
> based on the values they communicate. The
> leader must then live by them, in plain view of
> those he or she expects to follow the values.
> A leader must go beyond just talking about
> organizational values—such as "customers are
> always different"—they must actually demonstrate
> how to do this.

Casey understood that leading is not about telling others what to value and what to do. You have to model the way you want others to feel, think, and act. You have to show others that you are going to do exactly what you are asking them to do.

The Truth Is That You Either Lead by Example or You Don't Lead at All. In the second chapter of this book we revealed enduring leadership truth number two: *Credibility is the foundation of leadership.* At the end of our discussion of why credibility matters, we asked, "What is credibility behaviorally? How do you know it when you see it?" The most frequent answer we get in our research is: You have to *Do What You Say You Will Do*, or DWYSYWD for short.

There're lots of other common phrases for DWYSYWD. Walk the talk, practice what you preach, put your money where your mouth is, and follow through on your promises are some common ones. They all mean the same thing. Your actions had better be consistent with your words. In the final analysis, people believe what you do over what you say. As journalist and author Alan Deutschman writes in his book *Walk the Talk*, "Leaders have only two tools at their disposal: what they say and how they act. What they say might be interesting, but how they act is always crucial."[2]

Being interesting might be a goal for some leaders, and there's nothing wrong with that. It's beneficial to your brand to stand out from the crowd. But you'd best be more concerned about being believable before you work on being interesting. The world is full of interesting leaders who've been ousted once their character has been tarnished by their superficiality or misdeeds.

"Actions speak louder than words" is wise counsel to live by. Quite often the greatest distance that leaders have to travel is the distance from their mouths to their feet. Taking that step toward fulfilling a promise, putting the resources behind a pledge, and acting on a verbal commitment may require great courage. But it's the very thing that demonstrates the courage of your convictions.

SEEING IS BELIEVING

The truth of leading by example is accepted worldwide. It's ancient wisdom. For example, there's an old Chinese proverb that says, "The lower beam will not be level if the upper one is not." If you want others to behave in ways that are consistent with shared values and beliefs, you'd better make sure your beam is level.

Jack Li described his experience with this axiom when he was managing a small engineering service firm. As he tried to shift the team's business focus more toward service quality and customer satisfaction, he found out first-hand that "If the leader doesn't set a good example, nobody will believe what he/she says, and even if they believe, they won't know how to follow." While he communicated this with his team and they agreed in theory, the challenge was how to make it happen.

Jack and his team held several meetings in which they defined what service quality and customer service meant. They made a list of important criteria, such as assurance, reliability, responsiveness, flexibility, and empathy. They then established measurable performance indicators for the projects based on these guidelines. Even with all this work, the team was still not clear about Jack's expectations. "Seeing is believing," Jack said, and his management team recognized that they had to set the example themselves and show the entire team how to deliver excellent service quality and create a high customer satisfaction experience.

Jack decided to personally take on a pilot project, and he organized several meetings to show the team step-by-step how to deliver the kind of service he was expecting. He went out to customer sites with team members, supported them as they made presentations on the project, and encouraged them to challenge each other so they could really get to the root of any project problems. Jack also offered his observations on what he heard and saw in the meetings, linking his comments to the key performance indicators they'd agreed on.

Jack discovered from all this that it wasn't simply the buzzwords and jargon, like service quality and customer satisfaction, that were important. He learned that it was vital for him to demonstrate what these words meant in practice. It was critical that he, as their leader, put them into action. He was a role model for the values, standards, and behaviors that he was expecting from others.

Research clearly substantiates the power of example. Cornell professor Tony Simons has investigated the "behavioral integrity"—his term for doing what you say you will do—of managers and has found that organizations "where employees strongly believe [that] their managers followed through on promises and demonstrated the values they preached were substantially more profitable than those whose managers score average or lower" on being role models.[3] Similarly, UCLA Professor

Donna McNeese-Smith found in her research studies that "If managers want productive employees, they must set a good example and practice what they preach."[4]

What's true for business is equally true in other sectors. Neil Kucera told us that when he was a summer counselor at Camp Hope (for abused children), he realized that "When you are in a group with a common purpose you need to look at each other as models." Neil found that while leadership may come in different forms, it "is mostly the model you provide for your peers in how you behave that makes the most difference." For example, he explained that "we seldom told the kids how to behave, we simply showed them an example, and it was contagious. The kids were always watching us, how we acted, and then mimicking our behavior."

That's the point. What Neil and other leaders have learned is that people are always watching. They're watching what you do and comparing it to what you say. When people see you doing what you say, then they have the evidence that you mean it. Otherwise it's just words. Your actions send the loudest signals about what other people should be doing.

LEADERS GO FIRST

As the manager of JMTek's procurement department, Penny Zhang became acutely aware of how important her own example was to her team when her company struggled to stay afloat during the worldwide economic meltdown in 2009. Her team in particular was under great pressure from the sales department to quickly fill and ship orders to customers. Penny first had to come to terms herself with what she felt was "the demanding and somewhat abusive behavior" her team was receiving, and secondly, how she was going to keep her team's morale high under all this pressure. Acknowledging that it might have been a lot easier to simply rant and rave back at the sales department, she realized that before she could ask others to change their attitudes and behavior, she had to be willing to do the same herself.

She understood that it would be only through her actions that people would come to know the depth of her convictions. So Penny shared her feelings with everyone on her team about how they needed to work together with the sales department, that they needed to appreciate how sales was under even more pressure than they were, and that, ultimately, everyone had to work together as a team. As a result of these revelations, Penny said:

> I began to change and act differently. I stopped complaining about sales and worked at being more upbeat. My subordinates could feel my positive influence; they also worked harder than before and learned to put themselves in our sales team's shoes. And as we complained less about sales,

our performance got better and we got fewer
complaints from our sales department.

Penny's lesson of "I learned that I must change myself
first and let others see me and then they will know how to
follow" is what every aspiring leader needs to appreciate.
People look to you to set the example. As their leader,
they expect you to be a role model for how they should
behave, how they should use their time, set priorities,
treat one another and customers, and a host of other
critical behaviors.

People become cynical, disenchanted, and downright
weary when leaders back away from or don't do what
they are asking of others. Over and over again the leaders
we interviewed said to us, "I couldn't ask others to do
something I was unwilling to do myself." Mary Godwin
became acutely aware of this when she was vice president of operations of a company that creditors were
threatening to put into bankruptcy. At first, Mary was
trying to figure out how she was going to keep herself
from resigning, never mind keep the operations team
together while the company worked its way out of debt.
Acknowledging that it would have been a lot easier to
leave, she explained, "It came to me that if I wanted
everyone else to be committed, then I had to be totally,
100 percent, without doubt, committed personally."

Mary realized that before she could ask others to
change she had to be willing to make those same changes

and sacrifices herself. What's more, she understood that it would be only through keeping her promises that people would come to know the depth of her convictions. "I had to follow through on commitments and show others by my actions how serious I was. My credibility depended upon this, and so I had to set the example for others to follow."

A big part of being seen as credible is keeping your promises. When you give your word that you'll do something, and then you follow through on your commitments, it has a powerful effect on people. Consider what it meant when Robert Kramer, an elementary school principal, kept his promise. He told the kids that if they read five thousand books over the fall that he would pitch a tent on the roof of the school and spend the weekend up there. Parents talked about how the idea made their children more excited about reading. By the end of the school term, the students in Kramer's school had read more than the required number of books. They met the principal's goal, and he made good on his word. He camped out on the roof.

"I was so happy that he kept his promise," said one eight-year-old student, as she stared up wide-eyed at her principal, up on the roof equipped with a tent, lawn chair, and some favorite books. "He's the best principal the school has ever had," exclaimed a mother of another student.[5] Want to be the best leader your organization has ever had? Be true to your word.

ADMIT YOUR MISTAKES

Nothing undermines or erodes your credibility and your effectiveness as a role model faster than not being willing to acknowledge and take responsibility when you've made a mistake. According to Kirk Hanson, executive director of the Markkula Center for Applied Ethics at Santa Clara University, this is the "Achilles' heel" of leaders: Believing that they know it all and, accordingly, believing that they will never fail.[6] Leaders make mistakes, mess up, and speak out on occasions when they should keep their mouths shut. Like the rest of us, leaders are only human. It's when you think that you're better than other people that you get yourself into such deep trouble that others don't even want to be in your presence, let alone follow you.

When you ask people what it means for a leader to be honest, their immediate response is that "she tells the truth" or that "he doesn't lie." The more reflective response—and crucial insight—is: "They're willing to admit when they are wrong. I know that they are capable of being honest with me when they say they made a mistake." Think about that. If you want others to perceive you as being honest, it's not just about telling the truth when it's easy. The more revealing test is telling the truth when it's difficult, even embarrassing and possibly damaging, to do so. Admitting you're wrong or that you don't know are some of the best signs that a leader can be believed.

Angelika Mehta, while a project manager at Computer Sciences Corporation, found this out for herself:

> When I made a mistake, I didn't hide it. For example, after a busy week and some long nights, I miscalculated the remaining budget and posted it on the whiteboard. I only realized my mistake a few days later. I let the team know right away about my mistake and they appreciated my honesty. I think this made it easier for them to admit to me when they made mistakes or had issues.

The lesson Angelika conveyed to her team was that "It is okay to make mistakes because you are human. Just admit your mistakes and do what you can to correct them and move on."

Moreover, a willingness on your part to admit mistakes sets a positive example for others. By showing others that you're willing to acknowledge that you've screwed up, you make it easier and permissible for others to do the same. You're also sending the signal that it's okay to take chances, prosper from mistakes, and grow and develop in the process.

If your mistakes create problems for others and not just for you, you also need to apologize. It's an important step in rebuilding any damage done to your credibility.

An apology lets others know that you are concerned about the impact of your behavior on them. You should also take quick action to rectify the situation. It never pays to postpone fixing the problem. If something isn't done immediately, matters can get worse. And sometimes, if your mistake causes undue hardship, you should make amends—meaning you may need to impose on yourself some kind of consequence that makes you suffer. One of the reasons for the populist anger against the leaders of financial institutions following the great recession of 2009 was that those in leadership positions were perceived as not only not losing anything as a result of risky behavior, but of actually receiving bonuses for violating a public trust. And the final thing that you need to do is attend to reactions others are having to your efforts to restore credibility. Attentiveness enables you to determine whether what you are doing is helping or is insufficient. These steps are all part of holding yourself accountable for the decisions you make, the actions you take, and the impact you have on others.

Another way in which you can hold yourself accountable is to seek and accept feedback. Feedback is vital to every self-correcting system, and it's vital to the growth and development of leaders. However, we've found in our research that asking for feedback is not all that easy for leaders to do. On the *Leadership Practices Inventory*—our 360-degree leadership assessment tool—the statement on which leaders consistently score the lowest is "asks for feedback on how my actions affect other people's performance."[7] In other words, the behavior that leaders and their constituents consider to be the weakest is the behavior that most enables leaders to know how they're doing! How can you learn very much if you're unwilling to find out more about how your behavior is impacting the behavior and performance of those around you? The short answer is: "You can't." It's your job as a leader to keep asking others, "How am I doing?" If you don't ask, they're not likely to tell you.

That's why Casey Harbin, account manager at Apple, told us she needed "to set aside time, even a few minutes each day, to reflect on something that bothered me or that I did well, so that I can both move on and move forward. Reflecting in this manner also helps me learn about other people and appreciate the impact that I have on them, and vice versa." Stan Anders, managing partner in Silicon Valley for KPMG, reinforces Casey's comment when he bluntly asks, "At the end of the day, can you say to yourself that you acted in concert with your values?" It's in these moments of reflection that you develop yourself and make sure that your behavior and actions are aligned with your values, sending clear signals to others about what's expected of everyone on the team.

Armed with information about how your behavior affects others, and with a willingness to acknowledge your shortcomings and mistakes, you will have the seed capital for growth and development. This is an antidote to hubris. It keeps you humble while at the same time making you more robust as a person.

—————

The Truth Is That You Either Lead by Example or You Don't Lead at All. Seeing is believing, and your constituents have to see you living out the standards you've set and the values you profess. You need to go first in setting the example for others. That's what it takes to get others to follow your lead. A big part of leading by example is keeping your promises. Your word is only as good as your actions. You have to realize that others look to you and your actions in order to determine for themselves how serious you are about what you say, as well as understand what it will mean for them to be "walking the talk." Your statements and actions are visible reminders to others about what is or is not important. And when you make a mistake, admit it. Admitting your mistakes and shortcomings goes a long way toward building up people's confidence in your integrity. It gives them one more important reason to put their trust in you.

THE BEST LEADERS ARE THE BEST LEARNERS

The potential to lead exists in you. If you apply your head, your heart, and your courage, you can learn to lead.

Remember what Melissa Poe Hood told us back in the first chapter? "Everything you need to be a successful leader you already have: your intelligence to see an issue and a way to fix it, your heart to stay motivated, and your courage not to give up," she said. "You can't look for the man behind the curtain to solve your concerns. Everything you need you already have."[1]

You need to believe this. Not everyone does, but you need to if you're going to become the best leader you can be. As technologically advanced as our world is, there still persists an insidious myth that leadership is reserved

for only a lucky few who genetically inherit the trait.
We are confronted with it nearly every time we give
a speech or conduct a workshop when someone asks,
"Are leaders born or made?"

Our answer? We've never met a leader who wasn't
born! We've also never met an accountant, artist, athlete,
engineer, lawyer, physician, writer, or zoologist who
wasn't born. We're all born. That's a given. It's what you
do with what you have before you die that makes the
difference.

Let's get something straight. Leadership is not preor-
dained. It is not a gene, and it is not a trait. There is no
hard evidence to support the assertion that leadership
is imprinted in the DNA of only some individuals and
that the rest of us missed out and are doomed to be
clueless.

**The Truth Is That the Best Leaders Are the Best
Learners.** Leadership can be learned. It is an observable
pattern of practices and behaviors, and a definable set
of skills and abilities. Skills can be learned, and when
we track the progress of people who participate in
leadership development programs, we observe that they
improve over time.[2] They learn to be better leaders as
long as they engage in activities that help them learn
how.

But here's the rub. While leadership can be learned,
not everyone learns it, and not all those who learn
leadership master it. Why? Because to master leadership

you have to have a strong desire to excel, you have to believe strongly that you can learn new skills and abilities, and you have to be willing to devote yourself to continuous learning and deliberate practice. No matter how good you are, you can always get better.

LEARNING IS THE MASTER SKILL

We've heard and read the stories of thousands of ordinary people who have led others to get extraordinary things done. When we ask people to tell us about a time when they have been at their best as leaders, every single person has a story to tell. It's not the absence of leadership ability or potential that inhibits the development of more leaders; it's the persistence of the myth that leadership can't be learned. This debilitating untruth is a far more powerful deterrent to your leadership development than your individual nature or the basics of the leadership process.

Over the years we've conducted a series of empirical studies to find out whether leaders could be differentiated by the range and depth of learning tactics they employ. We've wanted to know if how leaders learned played a role in how effective they were in leading. The results have been most intriguing. First, we found that leadership can be learned in a variety of ways. It can be learned through active experimentation, observation of others, study in the classroom or reading books, or simply reflecting on one's own and others' experiences.[3] Certain styles contribute to more effectiveness in some practices, but there is no one best style for learning everything there is to know. The style is not the thing.

What was more important was the extent to which individuals engaged in whatever style worked for them. Those leaders who were more engaged in each of their learning styles, regardless of what their styles were, scored higher on The Five Practices of Exemplary Leadership®.[4] The best leaders turned out to be the best learners.

These findings also raise an extremely interesting and mostly unexplored question: Which comes first, learning or leading? Whenever we ask our clients this question, their hunches are the same as ours. Learning comes first. When people are predisposed to be curious and want to learn something new, they are much more likely to get better at it than those who don't become fully engaged.

Learning is the master skill. When you fully engage in learning—when you throw yourself whole-heartedly into experimenting, reflecting, reading, or getting coaching—you are going to experience the thrill of improvement and the taste of success. More is more when it comes to learning.

We're not the only ones who find a strong correlation between engagement in learning and leadership effectiveness. Researchers Bob Eichinger, Mike Lombardo, and Dave Ulrich report that in their studies the single best predictor of future success in new and different managerial jobs is learning agility.[5] "Learning agility," as they define it, "is the ability to reflect on experience and then engage in new behaviors based on those reflections." And they go on to say, "Learning agility requires self-confidence to honestly examine oneself, self-awareness to seek feedback and suggestions, and self-discipline to engage in new behaviors."[6]

You have to have a passion for learning in order to become the best leader you can be. You have to be open to new experiences and open to honestly examining how you and others perform, especially under conditions of uncertainty. You have to be willing to quickly learn from your failures as well as your successes and to find ways to try out new behaviors without hesitation. You won't always do things perfectly, but you will get the chance to grow.

ADOPT A GROWTH MINDSET

Another dynamic that gives rise to the need for aspiring leaders to be first-rate learners is the astounding pace of change in the world. Not only do you have to be able to learn, but you have to learn how to learn, constantly absorbing and teaching yourself new ways of doing old things and new ways of doing new things. According to *New York Times* columnist and bestselling author Thomas Friedman:

> This is an ability every worker should cultivate in an age when parts or all of many jobs are constantly going to be exposed to digitization, automation, and outsourcing, and where new jobs, and whole new industries, will be churned up faster and faster. In such a world, it is not only what you know but how you learn that will set you apart. Because what you know today will be out-of-date sooner than you think.[7]

Building your capacity to be a lifelong and agile learner begins with what Stanford psychologist Carol Dweck refers to as a growth mindset. "The growth mindset," she says, "is based on the belief that your basic qualities are things you can cultivate through your efforts."[8] Individuals who have a growth mindset believe people can learn to be better leaders—that they are made and not born.

Carol compares this to a *fixed mindset*—"believing that your qualities are carved in stone."[9] Those with the fixed mindset think leaders are born and that no amount of training is going to make you any better than you naturally are.

If you buy into the view that leaders are born and that talents are fixed at birth, it is highly unlikely that you'll put forth the time and effort to be better than you already are. You'll just wait for your talents to naturally blossom. On the other hand, if you begin with the belief that you can learn new skills no matter your present level of performance and that training and development will pay off, then you're much more likely to do what it takes to improve.

Mindsets carry over into performance. In study after study, researchers have found that, when working on simulated business problems, those individuals with fixed mindsets gave up more quickly and performed more poorly than those with growth mindsets.[10] The same is true for kids in school, athletes on the playing field, teachers in the classroom, and partners in relationships.[11] Mindsets and not skill sets make the critical difference in taking on challenging situations.

These findings may seem like heresy in this day and age, when there is so much emphasis on talent, but they are nonetheless true. As Carol says:

> People who believe in the power of talent tend
> not to fulfill their potential because they're so
> concerned with looking smart and not making
> mistakes. But people who believe that talent
> can be developed are the ones who really push,
> stretch, confront their own mistakes, and learn
> from them.[12]

We would be the first to argue that coaching can facilitate leadership development, but the stark reality is that a leader's mindset, fixed or growth, significantly impacts his or her inclination to lead. It seems the first thing that you need to accept is that you can learn to lead. When you believe that you can learn, then you will. And then, when you see that you can learn, you'll realize that others can also learn to lead. Your belief in your own capacity to lead not only benefits you; it also benefits all your constituents.

DELIBERATE PRACTICE IS REQUIRED

A mid-career executive in one of our leadership seminars recently shared this observation. He started by recalling an address given to him and his classmates at the Naval Academy in 1992 by General Colin Powell: "The General told the assembled Brigade of Midshipmen that one of the tenets of a good leader is to never stop learning. He stressed that we must use every experience, good or bad, to strengthen our leadership identity." He went on to say, "Among the leadership lessons I learned, the impact of making time for practicing good leadership strikes me as the most significant." You can't learn to be a good leader without putting in the time and practice.

Florida State University professor and noted authority on expertise K. Anders Ericsson makes this same point:

> Until most individuals recognize that sustained training and effort is a prerequisite for reaching

expert levels of performance, they will continue
to misattribute lesser achievement to the lack of
natural gifts, and will thus fail to reach their own
potential.[13]

Anders and his colleagues have found, over the
twenty-five years of their research, that raw talent is
not all there is to becoming a top performer. It doesn't
matter whether it's in sports, music, medicine, computer
programming, mathematics, or other fields: Talent is not
the key that unlocks excellence.

Staggeringly high IQs don't characterize the great
performers either. Sometimes they are really brilliant,
but in many instances they're just average. Similarly,
years of experience don't necessarily make someone a
high performer, let alone the greatest performer. And,
as startling as it might sound, sometimes more years of
experience can mean poorer performance compared to
those newly graduated in a specialty.

What truly differentiates the expert performers from
the good performers is hours of practice. You've got to
work at becoming the best, and it sure doesn't happen
over a weekend. If you want a rough metric of what
it takes to achieve the highest level of expertise, the
estimate is about 10,000 hours of practice over a period
of ten years.[14] That's about 2.7 hours a day, every day,
for ten years!

When we asked Glenn Michibata, head coach of
men's tennis at Princeton University, how much time

his players practiced every day, Glenn responded, "I tell them they need to practice two hours every day if they want to stay the same; more if they want to get better." On another occasion, we had the opportunity to pose that question to Lang Lang, the young Chinese piano virtuoso and music world phenomenon. He told us that for the first fifteen years—he started playing the piano at age two-and-a-half—he practiced for six to eight hours a day. Now, as a professional, he practices three hours a day, every day.

Both Lang's and Glenn's responses illustrate what researchers document. You won't find a fast track to excellence. There's no such thing as instant expertise. There's no shortcut to greatness in leadership or anything else. Those who are the very best became that way because they spent more time learning and practicing, not less time learning.

But it's not any kind of practice that works. "Living in a cave does not make you a geologist," Anders humorously observes, and simply being in a management position does not make you a great leader. Researchers are clear that not all practice makes perfect. You need a particular kind of practice—"deliberate practice"—to develop expertise.[15]

According to those who have extensively studied the subject, deliberate practice has five elements.[16] First, *it is designed specifically to improve performance*, which means there is a methodology and there is a very clear goal. If you want to become expert, you have to have an improvement target, a way to measure success, and a specific process for accomplishing the goal.

Secondly, *it has to be repeated a lot*. It must be done over and over and over again until it's automatic. That takes hours of repetition, during which you need to pay as much attention to the methodology as to the goal. Sloppy execution is not acceptable to top performers. This is one of the biggest problems with training and development these days. After a couple of weekend sessions, people move on to something new, or maybe nothing at all. There is little or no sustained effort to perfect a skill.

The third element of deliberate practice is that *feedback on results must be continuously available*. Every learner needs feedback. It's the only way you know whether or not you're getting close to your goal and whether or not you're executing properly. While there may come a time when you're accomplished enough to assess your own performance, it's always wise to bring in a coach, mentor, or some other third party to help you analyze how you did. You need an objective view, and you need someone who's not afraid to tell you the truth. Most people know intellectually that feedback is required, but are reluctant to make themselves vulnerable. They want to look good more than they want to get good!

Openness to feedback, especially negative feedback, is characteristic of the best learners, and it's something all leaders, especially aspiring ones, need to cultivate. Which was exactly the point Hilary Hall realized as she reflected upon her experience with us in our leadership seminar at the Hong Kong University of Science and Technology: "It can be somewhat of a painful and embarrassing experience to admit that there are parts of us that are unflattering, but it is a necessary component of self-reflection and growth." She was appreciating how "becoming a great leader takes practice and the willingness to view oneself with a critical eye."

The fourth element of deliberate practice is that *it is highly demanding mentally*. Developing expertise requires intense concentration and focus. Practice sessions need to be free of those daily interruptions that are commonplace in everyone's day-to-day routines. Deliberate practice is really difficult to do on the job. You need to find a way to turn off the electronic devices, close the door, and pay attention to learning. Additionally, the limiting factor in most practice sessions is often more mental than physical. You are more likely to tire from mental strain than from physical strain.

The final element of deliberate practice you must appreciate, sorry to say, is that *it isn't all that much fun*. While you should absolutely love what you do, deliberate practice is not designed to be fun. What keeps the top performers going during the often grueling practice sessions is not the fun that they're having, but the knowledge that they're improving and getting closer to their dream of superior performance. It's like they say in sports, "no pain, no gain." Save the fun for after the practice session.

SUPPORT HELPS

Studies of top performers strongly suggest that you have to have a supportive environment in order to develop expertise. A supportive family is very common in the stories of world-class performers. Supportive colleagues at work are critical. Leadership can't grow in a culture that isn't supportive of continuing development. Researchers have found, in fact, that when there are high-quality relationships at work—relationships characterized by positive regard for others and a sense of mutuality and trust—people engage in more of the behaviors that lead to learning.[17] You need to surround yourself with people who are going to offer you encouraging words when you try something new, understanding and patience when you fail, and helpful suggestions as you try to learn from mistakes.

Coaches, mentors, and teachers, while tough and demanding, are also common sources of support. Research shows that coaching is number two on the list of the most effective strategies for accelerating the development of high potentials.[18] Just as leaders can't lead alone, they can't learn alone either.

These days you hear a lot about how you should ignore your weaknesses, or you should find someone else who's good at what you aren't good at and partner with him or her. While it may be decent operational advice, that message is not consistent with what those who study expertise have found. Researchers have shown, across a variety of occupations and professions, that only by working at what you *cannot do* can you expect to become the expert you aspire to be.[19]

If you want to be the best leader you can be, you will have to attend to your weaknesses. You can't delegate or assign to others those skills you aren't good at. If you do, you'll only become as good as your weakest skill.

Melissa Guzy, managing director in Asia for Vantage Point Venture Partners, told us, "Just because you have a title doesn't mean you can step back and not develop yourself as a leader." You have to work at it, and Melissa maintained that you have to constantly educate yourself over time if you expect to lead and continue to be a leader. This requires, she said, "an obsession with lifelong learning when it comes to leadership." Indeed, she asserted that "leadership capability is the defining variable in our making investment decisions in new start-up ventures."

If you're thinking about starting your own organization or just improving the business you're in right now, learning to lead is an imperative. You have the capacity within you to do it, but you have to devote yourself to doing it every day.

————

The Truth Is That the Best Leaders Are the Best Learners. You can develop yourself as a leader, but it takes a continuous personal investment. It takes time, it takes deliberate practice, it requires setting improvement goals, staying open to feedback, working on your strengths and weaknesses, and having the support of others. Moreover, the very best leaders also believe that it's possible for everyone to learn to lead. By assuming that leadership is learnable, you stay open to opportunities to turn the workplace into a practice field and every experience into a chance to grow. By believing in yourself and your capacity to learn to lead, you make sure you're prepared to take advantage of the many opportunities that are open to you.

LEADERSHIP IS AN AFFAIR OF THE HEART

When you hear sportscasters talk about athletes who dig deep and make that extra effort that wins the match or the medal, they say, "He had a lot of heart." When you read news stories about someone who dedicated herself to something challenging, they often report, "It took a lot of heart." When you hear a story about someone who kept going despite all the odds, you say, "A lot of people would have given up. It took a lot of heart to do what she did." But you rarely, if ever, hear that said about managers. Why is that?

There's a prevailing myth that managers are supposed to divorce their emotions from a situation and approach things purely rationally. Every time you hear the phrase, "It's not personal, it's just business," you already know that the person has detached him- or herself from whatever he or she might be feeling. The trouble with this kind of advice is that it's completely misguided. Research indicates that the highest performing managers and leaders are the most open and caring. The best leaders demonstrate more affection toward others and want others to be more open with them. They are more positive and passionate, more loving and compassionate, and more grateful and encouraging than their lower performing counterparts.

The Truth Is That Leadership Is an Affair of the Heart. There's no integrity and honor without heart. There's no commitment and conviction without heart. There's no hope and faith without heart. There's no trust and support without heart. There's no persistence and courage without heart. There's no learning and risk taking without heart. Nothing important ever gets done without heart. Purely and simply, exemplary leaders excel at improving performance because they pay great attention to the human heart.

Author and educator Parker Palmer writes that "The power of authentic leadership . . . is found not in external arrangements but in the human heart. Authentic leaders in every setting—from families to nation-states—aim at liberating the heart, their own and others', so that its power can liberate the world."[1] Nothing external is going to save us. Not governments, not companies, not technologies, nor heroes on white horses. But imagine what can be done when people experience the power of the human heart.

LOVE IS THE SOUL
OF LEADERSHIP

Our friend and wise colleague Irwin Federman, former CFO, CEO, and currently with US Venture Partners, once said to us:

> You don't love someone because of who they are; you love them because of the way they make you feel. This axiom applies equally in a company setting. It may seem inappropriate to use words such as love and affection in relation to business. Conventional wisdom has it that management is not a popularity contest . . . I contend, however, that all things being equal, we will work harder and more effectively for people we like. And we like them in direct proportion to how they make us feel.

Your experience is likely to be similar to Irwin's. And yet, while it's almost taboo to talk about love and affection in an organizational context, when people describe their personal best leadership experiences it's not uncommon to hear them speak those words. There's a much deeper human connection when people are engaged with those they care about when doing things that really matter.

Love is the soul of leadership.[2] Love is what sustains people along the arduous journey to the summit of any mountain. Love is the source of the leader's courage. Leaders are in love: in love with leading, in love with their organizations' products and services, and in love with people.

The dictionary tells us that love is a "feeling of warm personal attachment or deep affection." In an organizational context, management consultant Rodney Ferris defines love as "a feeling of caring or deep respect for yourself and others, of valuing and believing in yourself and others, and of helping to achieve the best of which everyone is capable. It means finding a sense of purpose, fulfillment, and fun in your work, and helping others to find these qualities in their work as well."[3]

Exemplary leaders do not place themselves at the center; they place others there. They do not seek the attention of people; they give it to others. They do not focus on satisfying their own aims and desires; they look for ways to respond to the needs and interests of their constituents. "Servant leadership" is what many have called this relationship, wherein the task of leaders is to serve others.[4]

In our interview with Pete Thigpen, a senior fellow at The Aspen Institute and former president of Levi Strauss & Company USA, he reinforced this point when he advised leaders to:

> Really believe in your heart of hearts that your
> fundamental purpose, the reason for being, is
> to enlarge the lives of others. Your life will be

enlarged also. And all the other things we have been taught to concentrate on will take care of themselves.

Love enlarges lives. Love creates the desire to serve others and to see them grow and become their best. While constituents may initially be dependent on you for some benefit or gain, your end objective is to make them independent of you. We have repeatedly observed that, when working at their personal best, leaders transform their followers into leaders.

By understanding the needs and values of their constituents, exemplary leaders interact in ways that make others feel more confident and capable. They elevate people to a higher plane. They raise others' moral and ethical behavior, heighten positive emotions, elevate strategic thinking, enhance physical well-being, and generate significantly improved performance.

Gary Strack, former CEO of a regional health care system in Florida, told us that he strongly believed "the purpose of leadership was to create a legacy and not a legend." He went on to say:

> I constantly remind myself that my name is not on the organization. I think all leaders, including myself, need to be reminded of that and that we are just in our positions as stewards of our people and organizations which have been entrusted to us.

Self-centered managers can never achieve this kind of transformation. They're too focused on satisfying their own needs to be concerned about others. They're too concerned about becoming a legend and not leaving a lasting legacy. This explains why nearly 50 percent of administrative professionals say that having a "bad boss" would be the most important factor in a decision to leave their jobs. Compare that with only 4 percent who indicate that they would leave their jobs because of poor pay or the 2 percent who would leave because of poor benefits.[5] When you're around people who're more concerned about themselves than about you, you look for the nearest exit.

SHOW THEM THAT YOU CARE

It's not enough to *be* in love. As you know from personal experience, you have to show your love. That means you have to pay attention to your constituents, recognize them, and tell stories about them.

The primary way that you show that you care for someone is by paying attention to them. Giving your appreciation is an active process. You have to reach out to others, listen to their words and emotions, be open to their experiences, ask them questions, and express a willingness to learn from them. Making other people the center of your attention tells them that you feel they're important, it tells them that you regard their input as useful, and it tells them that you value their ideas.

Judith Wiencke, an engineering manager at Australia's Telecom, explains how...

> ... partnerships are created when my manager
> knows me and what I am all about, and in turn,
> I know the folks in my area and they know who I
> am as well. People appreciate knowing that I care
> about them and they seem to care more about what
> they're doing as a result.

Formal and informal recognitions are another visible way to show you care. They call attention to others' good work. This kind of appreciation is positive information that tells people they're making progress, are on the right track, and are living up to the standards. It also builds trust and a sense of shared contribution to success.

When Ying Qui was asked to become the principal of the primary school she was teaching at in Tongling, China, many people doubted her leadership ability. But as time progressed, she eventually doubled the size of the school's enrollment by getting the teachers to see how the success of the school connected to their own success. She worked hard at making everyone feel important and that they all made a difference. For the teachers who ranked at the top of their annual performance reviews, for example, the school publicly displayed their names and held a recognition event for them.

And what about everyone else? Ying explained: "We also had a number of special rewards for people who were making improvements." Caring about the people who worked in the school was critical, because Ying said: "It is a team, not 'me' but 'we,' and if everyone is supporting you, things will become much easier."

Recognitions don't need to come in the form of elaborate events or expensive awards. In fact, the more personal they are, the more impact they can have. William Hwang told us that he had "learned over the years that it isn't the size of the gesture that is important, but the simple fact that you noticed someone's contributions." At InnoWorks, the non-profit that he founded— an organization dedicated to opening the world of science, engineering, and medicine to underprivileged children—recognition ranges from acknowledgments in publicly distributed materials such as conference and journal papers, brochures, and the website, to simple *thank you's* in emails to the group.

Storytelling is another powerful way to show that you care. Stories exist in all organizations and are an integral part of defining what an organization is and what it means to work for it. Indeed, much about the culture of a company can be learned as a result of listening to and understanding the stories told about it.[6] Researchers have found, for instance, that organizational members who were able to tell many stories, particularly positive stories, exhibited far more evidence of organizational commitment and resilience from hardship than those who told few stories.[7] Similarly, storytelling boosts self-esteem in children, improving their interpersonal skills and resilience in the face of adversity.[8]

Lidia Kwiatkowska, personal banking area manager at Canada's Bank of Montreal/Harris, has experienced first-hand the power of sharing positive success stories about how lasting relationships are built through exceptional service. "Weekly," she says, "we share these stories, and how individual team members exhibit the customer attributes. We don't just celebrate, but challenge each other as a team." Before Lidia's arrival, her area hadn't achieved their revenue goals for several years, and within six months of her arrival they exceeded their targets for the entire year![9]

One of the most significant ways in which you can show others that you care and appreciate others' efforts is to be out there with them. Walk the halls, meander around the corridors, eat in the cafeteria, listen to complaints, go to parties, attend organizational events (even when you are not on the program), and be able to tell stories about their successes. This type of visibility and availability makes you more real, more genuine, more approachable, and more human. It helps you stay in touch with what's really going on.

That's what Carolyn Borne makes it a point to do in her three leadership roles at the UCLA Medical Center: unit director of the General Clinical Research Center, program director of the Women's Health Initiative, and Magnet director. For example, after leading the Medical Center to Magnet status—sometimes called the "Nobel Prize for Nursing"—she intentionally has kept the pride and momentum going by constantly thinking about others and what she can to do make their lives more rewarding. "I don't want them to lose the power of what they felt when we finally got Magnet," she told us. "I am constantly deliberating with them, talking with them, sensing them, finding out where they are, what they want, how they are feeling about the organization, and what they want me to bring to them."

Whether hard at work or over coffee, at lunch, or just "hanging out," Carolyn sees each encounter as an opportunity to show that she pays attention to each member of the team as an individual as well as a professional. "I hope that at the end of the day I've given my staff, or any of the people that I'm in contact with, the feeling that I cared about them."

FALL IN LOVE
WITH WHAT YOU DO

Leadership is tough and demanding work. There are a lot of successes and victories along the way, but there are also a lot failures and defeats. Leading takes considerable persistence and patience—and a lot of hours and energy. It's impossible to envision getting up day after day, putting in the long hours and hard work it takes to inspire, strengthen, and encourage others to get extraordinary things done, without having your heart in it.

When we asked Jim Autry, former president of Meredith Corporation's magazine group and author of several books on leadership—including the aptly titled *Love and Profit*—about the connection between these two words, he told us that "creating a caring workplace—a place in which people have friendships and deep personal connections and can grow personally and emotionally, psychologically and spiritually, as well as financially and professionally—is an important aspect of creating profit." As part of that process, Jim recommends,

> If you find that you're not liking what you're doing,
> you should fall in love with it. I started really liking
> to be a manager, but . . . it was only after devel-
> oping and evolving a way of doing things in a
> management style that came to be the love and
> profit style, the community-building style, that I
> could see extraordinary fruits.

To become the best leader you can be, you have to fall in love with the work you are doing and with the reason you are doing it. You have to fall in love with leading and the purpose you are serving. By "falling in love with leading" we don't mean the kind of covetous love that so many people get when they imagine what it'd be like to be *the leader* of something. They imagine how cool it'd be to be on top, to be in charge, to be able to get people to do things for them, to be famous, or to be wealthy. Leadership to them becomes one of those television reality shows where people connive and compete to win a million dollars. That's not what we're talking about. It only creates envy, jealousy, and greed.

We're talking about the kind of love that Stephen J. Dubner and Steven D. Levitt, authors of the bestselling book *Freakonomics*, write about when they say, "When it comes to choosing a life path, you should do what you love—because if you don't love it, you are unlikely to work hard enough to get very good."[10] We're talking about the same kind of love people feel when they have a passion for something, when they want to be the very best at something.

This is exactly the realization that Adam Carson, as vice president at Morgan Stanley, came to. "Everything that I have accomplished as a leader that I am most proud of," Adam told us, "has come when I was passionate about the role I was in and the organization that I belonged to. No question about it and this makes complete sense." As Adam explained:

> Looking back on the event, I truly believe that I got the job because of my passion and excitement. I carried that passion with me whenever I walked into a room for the next few months and the response was amazing. People were so

> interested in what I was teaching and talking about
> . . . not necessarily because they personally cared
> so much about the subject, but because they could
> see how deeply I cared. Being passionate enabled
> me to be a great leader. From this experience, I
> learned that I am at my best when I am passionate
> and care deeply about what I am doing.

When you're passionate about a profession or avocation, like Adam is, you wake up in the morning excited to be engaged in something that gets your juices flowing. You just can't wait to do it. You're devoted to learning more. You're eager to put in the hours to practice getting great at it.

Loving leading means that you're passionate about values and visions that make a difference, that you look forward every day to devoting your time to strengthening others and building teams, that you relish the chance to tackle a daunting challenge and search for new possibilities, and that you truly enjoy recognizing others for their contributions to the success of the enterprise. This is the work you must fall in love with.

PROMOTE THE POSITIVE

Claire Owen is founder and leader of vision and values for the SG Group, a medium-sized firm in London designed to meet the marketing and human resource recruitment needs of agencies and corporations. In one interview with Claire, she said to us: "If you are excited about the business, and if you are excited about where it is going and what is happening in it, then there is a buzz, a physical buzz. It's my job to create that kind of place."

Claire added, "You see that I get excited about things. When I do, people go, 'Well, Claire is excited by it, so I'm going to get excited by it. She believes in and she thinks it is going to be great—well I think it is going to be great.' That's really all I do."

Claire is a living example of how "enthusiasm is infectious." When she is excited and animated, other people get excited and animated. People have told us from the first day we started researching the characteristics of admired leaders that they want leaders like Claire. They want people who are positive and optimistic. They want leaders who are inspiring and full of hope for the future. It's part of what makes a leader credible. It's part of what attracts people to leaders in the first place.

Claire's experience illustrates the power of positive leadership. People feed off of their leaders' moods and their leaders' views of the world. Positive leadership breeds positive emotions.

This isn't conjecture. This is fact. Barbara L. Fredrickson, professor of psychology at the University of North

Carolina at Chapel Hill, has been studying positivity for more than twenty years. Her findings indicate that

> Positivity opens us up. The first core truth about positive emotions is that they open our hearts and our minds, making us more receptive and more creative.[11]

Positivity "broadens and builds," observes Barbara. It stretches our minds, helps us to see new possibilities, and expands our worldviews. In the research she and her colleagues have done, they've found that as positivity flows through us we see more options, and we become more creative and innovative. It's not just wild and crazy ideas, either. When feeling positive, managers are more accurate and more careful in making decisions. They're also more interpersonally effective.[12]

And that's not all. People who enjoy more positivity are better able to cope with adversities and are more resilient during times of high stress. They are also more likely to see the commonalities between themselves and others. These are certainly the kinds of outcomes that are needed in a world that has become more diverse and more adverse.

These findings are further supported by the work of researcher Marcial Losada and University of Michigan professor Emily Heaphy, who examined the performance of sixty top management teams engaged in annual business planning activities.[13] In their field research they discovered that they could distinguish high-performing, medium-performing, and low-performing teams based on the ratio of positive to negative statements exchanged in team meetings. Positive statements are those that are supportive, appreciative, helpful, approving, and complimentary. Negative statements are those that are critical, disapproving, contradictory, and cynical and the like. For the high performers the ratio of positive to negative was 5.61 to 1, for the medium performers it was 1.14 to 1, and for the low-performing teams it was .93 to 1. In other words, the more positive the groups, the better they performed. The more negative the groups, the worse they did.[14]

In related studies of other interpersonal relationships, investigators have found evidence that when people experience a ratio of at least three positive emotions to one negative, they are more likely to be lasting and healthy.[15] Whether the ratio is 5:1 or 3:1, the important point is that relationships—whether work, personal, or family—flourish when people experience more positive than negative emotions. Those who experience little or no positive emotion languish and often die.

At this point, you're thinking about the voices of some cynics you've heard say: "Come on. Get real. This is a tough, hard, cruel world. You can't just paint a happy face on our problems and make them go away." Of course you can't. Leaders shouldn't turn a blind eye to reality or hide it from their teams. You must be honest with your constituents about the state of the organization's or the nation's health. Then you have a choice.

You can tell people they're doomed, criticize the ideas they present, contradict them at every turn, and offer little or no support as they struggle to survive. Or you can give them hope. You can tell people that if they apply themselves—and if they're willing to struggle and suffer—they will overcome one day. You can tell them you have confidence in their abilities, help them to broaden their perspectives, build on their ideas, support them as they look for solutions, and recognize their contributions. It's not hard to recognize the right option to choose.

Positive energy is especially important in volatile times. When the news is worrisome, and often downright scary, it's pretty easy for folks to become negative. And people become negative even faster when they see it in their leaders, whether overtly in speeches or even if they just mope around a bit. Negative leadership breeds negative emotions. And these negative emotions are far more damaging to an organization's and an individual's health than doing nothing at all. In uncertain and challenging times, it's your obligation as a leader to accentuate the positive. If you don't, you're either keeping things the same or making them worse.

Call it the physics of leadership: positives attract, negatives repel. In order to get through the difficulties of today and tomorrow and to seek out opportunities, you have to believe that there is a positive future out there. It's imperative that leaders paint that attractive picture and generate the human energy necessary to enact it.

———

The Truth Is That Leadership Is an Affair of the Heart. Leaders put their hearts in their businesses and their businesses in their hearts. They love what they're doing and they stay in love with leading, with the people who do the work, with what their organizations produce, and with those who honor them by using their products and services. They show they care by paying attention to people, sharing success stories, and making people feel important and special. Exemplary leaders are positive and upbeat, generating the emotional energy that enables others to flourish.

LEADERS SAY YES

We began this book by saying that everything you will ever do as a leader is based on one audacious assumption: you matter. We now end this book with a similarly audacious proposition—that everything you do as a leader begins with one word: *yes.* Until you say yes, nothing great can happen.[1]

Take Ivana Sendecka, a young woman in Slovakia with a rather ambitious dream of wanting to prepare her country's next generation of leaders to embrace the future of Slovakia as their own.

Ivana's passion for leadership was evident very early in her life, when her dedication and skill earned her the role of captain on the Slovak Junior National Basketball Team for five years. It stayed with her in college where she pursued a master's degree in strategic management at the best business school in Slovakia—the Faculty of Management at Comenius University—and later as she adventurously relocated to Dubai for an internship experience, which then turned into three years of working there. But on a winter vacation back to Slovakia in 2007, Ivana realized that it was time to devote herself to the important work that needed to be done at home.[2]

Ivana left the Middle East and began a new quest in Bratislava, Slovakia, with a global consulting firm. In working with clients on team and organizational issues, Ivana discovered her love for leadership and personal development. She knew she wanted to "unleash talents in people, show them other perspectives in life and business, and [demonstrate] how via mindful leadership everyone can make a difference."

She also began to question the status quo around her and to challenge accepted norms. She wanted to know why, in a country with so many talented people, they were so shy in expressing their fullest potential. She saw reliable and trustworthy people who were delivering on-time quality work, but who didn't seem to have the confidence in their own abilities. She saw a generation of young people who were the first to grow up in a liberated country, but who had to work in a system that was held over from an older regime. She saw how her contemporaries were immigrating to other countries to get a better education, find better jobs, and make a decent living. She wanted to know what could be done to make her homeland more attractive to its own citizens, visitors, and most importantly to its next generation.

An avid social networker, Ivana began a series of online and Skype dialogues with her first mentor, Gary Haslam, on ways in which she could improve her own capacity to coach her clients and colleagues to become better leaders. Then she came across a book by Ron Carucci entitled *Leadership Divided*,[3] and even though she had never met Ron in person, she reached out to him on Facebook. (This is a very logical place for a Millennial to turn when wanting to connect with a new friend. It's also how we met Ivana for the first time.) The connection was almost immediate, and over the next few weeks Ivana and Ron collaborated on a document that would provide the architecture for developing emerging talent in Slovakia.

Ivana was so impassioned by her purpose and so committed to her cause, that she knew she had to devote all her time to it. She also learned she couldn't do this inside a large consulting firm, so she quit her job and set out on her own. She had no funding, no infrastructure, and, at first, no other people. She had only her passion, her persistence, and a very big dream.

In the face of the obstacles that every startup venture confronts, Ivana forged ahead. Her research revealed that despite the frustrations that were driving young Slovaks to want to leave the country, they had a deep hunger for creating something more vital in their homeland.

The challenge was how to help these emerging leaders believe that they could have thriving lives and careers while maintaining the uniqueness of their heritage in Slovakia. Ivana's generation had been raised under the communist flag of Czechoslovakia and were young when the borders opened and the country split into the Czech Republic and Slovakia. They now had the chance to define what it meant to be Slovak in a new nation. Were they up for this daunting task, or would they unwittingly perpetuate the passive, cynical legacy they so desperately wanted to flee?

After more online conversations with Ron, an idea was born: The Next Generation Leaders of Slovakia (NGLS). And an event was planned: The very first conference of NGLS, where young leaders would gather to share their hopes and envision the future of Slovakia. The effort took five months of virtual collaboration among a small team[4] and countless hours of hard work. It all paid off. On November 6, 2009, the doors opened to the first-ever NGLS conference, where more than one hundred emerging leaders began envisioning the future of Slovakia.

But it would not have happened had Ivana listened to the advice she was given four months prior.

In a conversation with a Slovak colleague whom she greatly respects, she was asked: "What do you want to do in life? What do you want your job to be like? What do you want to do for a living?" Ivana was so charged up at that moment that she responded very spontaneously:

> I really love coaching, I really love people, I love
> talking to people, I love interacting with people,
> unleashing the talents in them because I know it's
> possible from my own life experiences. I love to
> do workshops, I love to get people together and
> create something really mind-blowing. And use
> technology, use social media, give speeches; this
> is what I really love. I love people, and I really love
> showing them the purpose in life, how businesses
> can be improved, how we can be more human.
> This is what I'd love to do in life.[5]

Despite her personal enthusiasm, however, the response Ivana received was not at all encouraging. Her colleague told her that her dream was ridiculous, that she had no experience in anything that she mentioned, and that he wondered who would be listening to her. He questioned the viability of social technologies, saying they were a bubble that would soon burst. And he offered this analogy about her capabilities. He said to Ivana, "You are like a toy car. The world out there is like a Formula One, and you simply can't compete with Formula One if you are a toy car. So just forget it."

That would have been enough to stop most people in their tracks, and Ivana admits that there was a time when it would have done just that to her. But not this time. This time was different. This time, she said, "I just felt such a great, great energy deep inside me which I cannot describe, such a great faith in what I really want to do in life that nothing could stop me, no words, no people, nothing else."

Ivana walked out of that office and four months later the conference was born, where "amazing, amazing things happened." Participants talked and listened to each other, because they all cared about the future of their country. There were many tears, much laughter, and great creativity as these young leaders passionately wrote their "Stories from Tomorrow." "This was so new to them," Ivana told us. "No one had ever asked them what they thought. Before NGLS, they believed they had no say in their future—that it was just going to happen to them. Now this generation, so full of hope, ideas, talent, and passion, shared their dreams, learned a lot, and showed each other what they wanted to change."

When the conference was over, many expressed that they now believed in the future of Slovakia—and their part in that future. As one participant said, "I'd forgotten how to dream. You reminded me that I can dream, and how to dream, and that I must dream."

In reflecting on the lessons from her experience, Ivana offers this:

> No one will ever believe in you if you don't believe
> in yourself. First you have to start with yourself.
> Believe in your dreams, and don't let anyone tell

you that you cannot do it. You have got to protect
your dreams. You have got to fight for your dreams
and just live it because this is what life is for.

Ivana's belief in herself is what started her on the
path of fighting for her dreams, of venturing out into
unknown territory with nothing more than her inner
conviction and the courage to act on it.

REMINDERS ABOUT THE TRUTHS

We have come full circle. We began this book by talking
about the first truth about leadership—that you can
make a difference—and now Ivana brings us back to
where we started. Leadership begins when you believe
in yourself and that you can make a positive difference in
the world.

And yet Ivana's leadership experience is also a
reminder that others have to believe in you, too, and that
gaining followers can be tough and that it comes when
you work hard to earn their faith and confidence. The
truth is that credibility is the foundation of leadership.

You also see the power of the truth that values
drive commitment. You have to be clear about what's
important to you if you're going to devote yourself fully
to something. Further, Ivana's story illustrates the truth
that leaders focus on the future, whether it's the future of
a group, organization, nation, or the planet. Big dreams
that resonate with others inspire and energize.

The ways in which Ivana reached out to others for advice and consultation shows how true it is that you can't do it alone. While the leader may initially provide the spark of an idea, it takes a group of people—sometimes small and sometimes large—to make something extraordinary happen. And when beginning something brand new, the truth that trust rules is especially relevant. There isn't much else to go on. You just have to show that you trust others. Your trust in them will bring greater trust in you.

All leaders are severely tested, just as Ivana was, and there will always be detractors—those who will tell you it's impossible, that it can't be done, that you're not capable, and that your dream is foolish. The truth is that challenge is the crucible for greatness. Despite the obstacles and despite the naysayers, you just have to go out there and do it. You have to make mistakes, bounce back, and persist. And the truth is also that you either lead by example or you don't lead at all. You have to go first as a leader. You have to be the example that others can follow.

Further, this story makes evident the truth that the best leaders are the best learners. Whether it's from books, direct experience, consulting with others, using social technologies such as Facebook and Skype, or reflecting on the things that you do, learning is the master skill. And none of this would be possible if you don't love what you're doing and the people you're doing it with. The truth is that leadership is an affair of the heart. Love enlarges lives and love energizes leaders. You have to have a big heart to be a great leader.

The ten truths about leadership are apparent in the stories of the men and women who've shared their experiences in this book. We've also seen them in the thousands of other personal best leadership experiences we've heard over that last three decades. They reinforce how true it is that, while the context of leadership changes, the content of leadership endures. There are certain fundamentals that support everything that leaders do, and those essentials will continue to inform what leaders do long into the future.

And there is still one more truth that has to be added.

YOU ARE RESPONSIBLE

When we sent the manuscript pages of this book to Melissa Poe Hood so she could review her story for accuracy, she returned her edits and added this note:

> I do believe everyone struggles with life purpose; however, a leader is one who steps beyond her own self-doubts and realizes her journey is her responsibility. Whether one is a child or an adult, an individual participates in the world, and she should do so deliberately. Ultimately, the worst thing one can do is to see a problem and think it is someone else's responsibility.

Melissa reminds us all that leadership is not about wishful thinking. It's about determined doing. There are no shortages of problems and opportunities. They are evident at work, at home, in our communities, in our countries, and around the globe. There are no shortages of problems to solve. Leadership is not about telling others that they ought to solve these problems. It's about seeing a problem and accepting personal responsibility for doing something about it. And it's about holding yourself accountable for the actions that you take. The next time you see a problem and say "Why doesn't someone do something about this?" take a look in the mirror and say instead, "I'll be the someone to do something about it."

This doesn't mean that you have to accept responsibility for every problem, and it doesn't mean that you should solve it by yourself. What it does mean is that leaders aren't bystanders in the parade of life. They are active participants who work tirelessly to mobilize others to want to struggle for shared aspirations. Leaders believe that they have an obligation to do something to bring about change and that, with the active engagement of others, they can move things forward. As a leader you are entrusted with the hopes and dreams of others, and you will be called to account for the actions that you take.

Are you familiar with the riddle of the twelve frogs? It goes like this: Twelve frogs are sitting on a log. Twelve frogs decide to jump into the pond. How many frogs remain on the log?

The answer? Twelve. Twelve frogs remain on the log because there is a clear difference between deciding to jump and jumping. If you are going to lead, you not only have to decide, but you also have to make the leap.

In May 2009, University of Connecticut President Michael Hogan addressed graduating seniors at the university's commencement. He was speaking about the difficult economic times and how important it was to face hardship with courage and resourcefulness. He referred to some advice he heard from talk-show satirist and social commentator Stephen Colbert about how important it is to say "yes" when someone offers you a job. Though Colbert's comments were embedded in a humorous piece on how new graduates need to get jobs, any jobs, its core message was spot on for young men and women heading out into the world of work during a major recession. Then Michael added:

> So, drawing on Colbert, James Joyce, or Norman Vincent Peale, depending on your reading list, my first word of advice is this: Say 'yes.' And to summarize Colbert: "... say 'yes' as often as you can." Of course, saying 'yes' can lead to mistakes. So don't be afraid to make a mistake, because, as he continues, you can't be young and wise at the same time.

Saying 'yes' begins things. "Saying 'yes' is how
things grow." Saying 'yes,' he goes on, leads to
new experiences, and new experiences will lead
to knowledge and wisdom. "'Yes' is for young
people," Colbert concludes. And I agree. An atti-
tude of 'yes' is how you will be able to go forward
in these uncertain times.[6]

Michael's advice (and Stephen Colbert's, too) is
clearly appropriate for graduates seeking employment,
but it's also especially relevant for leaders seeking to
make change happen. You have to say yes to begin
things. You have to say yes to your beliefs, you have to
say yes to big dreams, you have to say yes to difficult
challenges, you have to say yes to collaboration, you have
to say yes to trust, you have to say yes to learning, you
have to say yes to setting the example, and you have to
say yes to your heart.

Are you ready to say yes to leadership? When you
are ready to say yes, doors will open to entirely new
adventures in your life. When you are ready to say yes,
people will join you on the quest. When you say yes, you
will discover your own truth about leadership.

ABOUT THE AUTHORS

Jim Kouzes and Barry Posner are co-authors of the award-winning, best-selling book, *The Leadership Challenge*. Since its first edition in 1987, *The Leadership Challenge* has sold nearly two million copies worldwide and is available in more than twenty-two languages. It has won numerous awards, including the Critics' Choice Award from the nation's book review editors and the James A. Hamilton Hospital Administrators' Book-of-the-Year Award, and was selected as one of the top ten books on leadership in *The Top 100 Business Books of All Time*.

Jim and Barry have co-authored more than a dozen other award-winning leadership books, including *A Leader's Legacy; Credibility: How Leaders Gain It and Lose It, Why People Demand It; Encouraging the*

Heart; The Student Leadership Challenge; and *The Academic Administrator's Guide to Exemplary Leadership.* They also developed the highly acclaimed *Leadership Practices Inventory* (LPI), a 360-degree questionnaire for assessing leadership behavior, which is one of the most widely used leadership assessment instruments in the world, along with *The Student LPI.* More than four hundred doctoral dissertations and academic research projects have been based on their Five Practices of Exemplary Leadership® model.

Among the honors and awards that Jim and Barry have received are the American Society for Training and Development's (ASTD) highest award for their Distinguished Contribution to Workplace Learning and Performance, and the Management/Leadership Educators of the Year award from the International Management Council. They were named among the Top 50 Leadership Coaches in the nation (according to *Coaching for Leadership*).

Jim and Barry are frequent speakers, and each has conducted leadership development programs for hundreds of organizations, including Apple, Applied Materials, ARCO, AT&T, Australia Post, Bank of America, Bose, Charles Schwab, Cisco Systems, Community Leadership Association, Conference Board of Canada, Consumers Energy, Dell Computer, Deloitte Touche, Dorothy Wylie Nursing Leadership Institute, Egon Zehnder International, Federal Express, Gymboree,

Hewlett-Packard, IBM, Jobs DR-Singapore, Johnson & Johnson, Kaiser Foundation Health Plans and Hospitals, L. L. Bean, Lawrence Livermore National Labs, Lucile Packard Children's Hospital, Merck, Motorola, NetApp, Northrop Grumman, Oracle, Petronas, Roche Bioscience, Siemens, Standard Aero, 3M, Toyota, the U.S. Postal Service, United Way, USAA, Verizon, VISA, Vodafone Hutchison Australia, and The Walt Disney Company.

Jim Kouzes is the Dean's Executive Professor of Leadership, Leavey School of Business, at Santa Clara University, and lectures on leadership around the world to corporations, governments, and non-profits. He is a highly regarded leadership scholar, an experienced executive, and *The Wall Street Journal* cited him as one of the twelve best executive educators in the United States. In 2010, Jim received the Thought Leadership Award from the Instructional Systems Association, the most prestigious award given by the trade association of training and development industry providers. In 2006 Jim was presented with the Golden Gavel, the highest honor awarded by Toastmasters International. Jim served as president, CEO, and chairman of the Tom Peters Company from 1988 through 1999, and prior to that led the Executive Development Center at Santa Clara University (1981–1987). Jim founded the Joint Center for

Human Services Development at San Jose State University (1972–1980) and was on the staff of the School of Social Work, University of Texas. His career in training and development began in 1969 when he conducted seminars for Community Action Agency staff and volunteers in the war on poverty. Following graduation from Michigan State University (B.A. degree with honors in political science), he served as a Peace Corps volunteer (1967–1969). Jim can be reached at jim@kouzes.com.

————

Barry Posner is professor of leadership at Santa Clara University, where he has received numerous teaching and innovation awards and served as dean of the Leavey School of Business for twelve years (1996–2009). An internationally renowned scholar and educator, Barry is author or co-author of more than one hundred research and practitioner-focused articles. He currently serves on the editorial review boards for *Leadership and Organizational Development, Leadership Review,* and *The International Journal of Servant-Leadership.* In 2011 he received the *Journal of Management Inquiry* Outstanding Scholar Award, which is given in recognition of outstanding contributions that have had major impacts on the field of management. A frequent speaker and workshop facilitator, Barry has also been a visiting professor at the University of Western Australia, Hong Kong University of Science and Technology, and Sabanci University (Turkey).

Barry received his baccalaureate degree with honors in political science from the University of California, Santa Barbara, his master's degree in public administration from The Ohio State University, and his doctoral degree in organizational behavior and administrative theory from the University of Massachusetts, Amherst. Having consulted with a wide variety of public- and private-sector organizations around the globe, Barry also works at a strategic level with a number of community-based organizations, currently sitting on the board of directors of EMQ Family First. He has served previously on the board of the American Institute of Architects (AIA), Junior Achievement of Silicon Valley and Monterey Bay, San Jose Repertory Theater, Public Allies, Big Brothers/Big Sisters of Santa Clara County, the Center for Excellence in Nonprofits, Sigma Phi Epsilon Fraternity, and several start-up companies. Barry can be reached at bposner@scu.edu.

ACKNOWLEDGMENTS

The truth is that **you can't do it alone**. It's true for leaders, and it's also true for authors. Every time we work on a new book we're reminded of how much others contribute to what you read between the covers.

We wouldn't ever have been able to begin this journey without all the leaders who've shared their inspiring stories with us. Their experiences bring the text to life. They make it breathe and give it real-world relevance. Over the years, we've gathered thousands of case examples, and in this book there are over fifty folks who've opened themselves up to us. We very much appreciate their willingness to make themselves available to us, and to you.

When we first began work on this book, we convened a small group of emerging leaders to advise us. In a series of live and virtual conversations, Miles Ashlock, Daren Blonski, and Amanda Crowell Itliong stimulated our thinking and offered crucial insights into the challenges facing the next generation of leaders. We are grateful to them for their dedication to developing the leaders of the future.

We want to extend a special thank you to Stephen DeKrey, senior associate dean of the Business School at the Hong Kong University of Science and Technology. He provided Barry with the opportunity to serve as a visiting professor in the fall of 2009. It was there that we were able to expand our global view of leadership and gain insight into the diverse lives of those who reside in places far from our homes in California.

Then there are our good colleagues at John Wiley & Sons. We've been working together for twenty-five years now, and we know there are more great years ahead. Karen Murphy, our senior editor at Jossey-Bass, was the driving force behind *The Truth About Leadership*. She has challenged us, encouraged us, and supported us throughout the entire process. We are grateful for her confidence, her expertise, and her perseverance. We would not have started this book, let alone finished it, without her mostly gentle and resolute encouragement to persist. Mark Karmendy, editorial production manager, ensured that the book made it from manuscript to printed pages. Our copy editor, Rebecca Taff, applied her writing craft, making sure this is an enjoyable experience for our readers. We give a shout out to Gayle Mak, senior editorial assistant, for the important part she played in keeping us connected and on schedule. Without Carolyn Carlstroem, marketing manager, and Amy Packard, publicity manager, you wouldn't know about this book—or any of our others. Books have to be noticed on the shelves, on the Internet, and in the media, and they do an awesome job of getting the word out. Thanks to Adrian Morgan, art director, for creating the attractive and eye-catching jacket and making the interior look and feel just right. Lisa Shannon, associate publisher at Pfeiffer, another Wiley imprint, always deserves special thanks, and hugs, for her role as chief strategist and cheerleader of *The Leadership Challenge* suite of products. We are eternally grateful to John Wiley & Sons for its enthusiastic support of our work. Two executives, in particular, have been our champions for decades now. A big, big thank you to Cedric Crocker, vice president and publisher, and Debra Hunter, president, Jossey-Bass and Pfeiffer imprints.

At the beginning of each day when we begin our work, and at the end of the day when we shut down the computer for a little rest, there are really only two people who are always there for us. We are blessed with the loving support, generous encouragement, helpful feedback, and constructive coaching of our spouses, Tae Kouzes and Jackie Schmidt-Posner. They've sacrificed much so that we could devote just a few more minutes to this book ... and many others. We are very lucky guys to have such extraordinary partners. We also want to thank Nicholas Lopez, Jim's son, and Amanda Posner, Barry's daughter, for the inspiration they've given us. They were constantly on our minds as we reflected on the hopes and dreams of a new generation of men and women in the workplace. With these very special people in our lives, it drives home how true it is that leadership is an affair of the heart.

We also want to acknowledge that, without you, our readers, we'd never be able to make a contribution beyond the perimeter of our immediate friends and family. We greatly appreciate how you have accepted us into your organizational families, and we thank you for the opportunity to join with you in leaving this world a little bit better than we found it.

———

Jim Kouzes
Orinda, California
July 2010

Barry Posner
Santa Clara, California
July 2010

NOTES

TRUTH ONE

1. Private correspondence with Melissa Poe Hood dated January 22, 2010. Also, "Melissa Poe," *Caring People (6)*, Fall 1993: 66, supplemented by interview with Trish Poe on November 3, 1994. See also James M. Kouzes and Barry Z. Posner, *The Leadership Challenge, 3rd Edition*. San Francisco, CA: Jossey-Bass, 2002, pp. 209–210. For more information on Kids F.A.C.E., see the website, www.kidsface.org.

2. Melissa Poe, "A Club of Six," Kids F.A.C.E. website, http://www.kidsface.org/pages/aclubofsix.html, accessed January 19, 2010.

3. Speech at 2009 Women of Distinction ceremony, June 4, 2009. A video of her speech can be found on YouTube, at http://www.youtube.com/watch?v=8QMyECutpQo.

4. LPI Data Analysis, www.theleadershipchallenge.com.

5. This survey was first conducted in 1998 for Public Allies, now a part of AmeriCorps, only to those eighteen to thirty-two years of age. We adapted the survey and have administered it to a wider range of ages. See Public Allies, *New Leadership for a New Century* (Washington, DC: Public Allies, 1998).

6. James M. Kouzes and Barry Z. Posner, *Leadership Practices Inventory (LPI), 3rd Edition.* San Francisco: Pfeiffer, 2003.

7. James M. Kouzes and Barry Z. Posner, *The Leadership Challenge, 4th Edition.* San Francisco: Jossey-Bass, 2007. For more information about the impact of leaders on their constituents and organizations, visit our website for reports by the authors on their analysis of over one million responses to the *Leadership Practices Inventory* and abstracts on more than four hundred doctoral dissertations and other academic research. Here's the link: http://www.leadershipchallenge .com/WileyCDA/Section/id-131060.html.

8. Marianne Williamson, *A Return to Love: Reflections on the Principles of a Course in Miracles.* New York: HarperCollins, 1992, pp. 190–191.

TRUTH TWO

1. For more information about the original studies, see B. Z. Posner and W. H. Schmidt, "Values and the American Manager: An Update," *California Management Review*, 26(3), 1984, pp. 202–216; and B. Z. Posner and W. H. Schmidt, "Values and Expectations of Federal Service Executives," *Public Administration Review*, 1986, 46(5), pp. 447–454.

2. The classic study on credibility goes back to C. I. Hovland, I. L. Janis, and H. H. Kelley, *Communication and*

Persuasion (New Haven, CT: Yale University Press, 1953); and early measurement studies including J. C. McCroskey, "Scales for the Measurement of Ethos," *Speech Monographs* 33 (1966), pp. 65-72, and D. K. Berlo, J. B. Lemert, and R. J. Mertz, "Dimensions for Evaluating the Acceptability of Message Sources," *Public Opinion Quarterly, 3* (1969), pp. 563-576. However, even further back, Aristotle (384-322 B.C.), writing in *Rhetoric*, suggested that Ethos, the Trust of a speaker by the listener, or what some have referred to as "source credibility," was based on the listener's perception of three characteristics of the speaker: the intelligence of the speaker (correctness of opinions or competence), the character of the speaker (reliability—a competence factor—and honesty—a measure of intentions), and the good will of the speaker (positive energy and favorable intentions toward the listener). These three characteristics (competence, honesty, and inspiration) have consistently emerged in factor-analytic investigations of communicator credibility (D. J. O'Keefe, *Persuasion: Theory and Research* [Thousand Oaks, CA: Sage, 2002]). Another contemporary perspective is provided in R. Cialdini, *Influence: The Psychology of Persuasion* (New York: Collins, 2007).

3. James M. Kouzes and Barry Z. Posner, *Credibility: How Leaders Gain and Lose It, Why People Demand It.* San Francisco: Jossey-Bass, 2003.

TRUTH THREE

1. B. Z. Posner and W. H. Schmidt, "Demographic Characteristics and Shared Values," *International Journal of Value-Based Management,* 1992, 5(1), pp. 77-87. See also

B. Z. Posner, "Another Look at the Impact of Personal and Organizational Values Congruency," *Journal of Business Ethics*, in press.

2. Paul Polman interview with Adam Bird, *McKinsey Quarterly*, October 2009.

3. David Whyte, *The Heart Aroused: Poetry and the Preservation of the Soul in Corporate America.* New York: Doubleday Currency, 2002, p. 143.

4. James M. Kouzes and Barry Z. Posner, *The Leadership Challenge Workshop Values Cards.* San Francisco: Pfeiffer, 2010.

TRUTH FOUR

1. Elliot Jaques, who has written extensively about future orientation. See, for example, Elliott Jaques, *Requisite Organization: The CEO's Guide to Creative Structure and Leadership.* Arlington, VA: Cason Hall and Company, 1989, pp. 15–32.

2. Gary Hamel and C. K. Prahalad, *Competing for the Future: Breakthrough Strategies for Seizing Control of Your Industry and Creating the Markets of Tomorrow.* Cambridge, MA: Harvard Business School Press, 1996, pp. 3–4.

3. Michael Hyatt, "Why Vision Matters." Posted December 16, 2009; retrieved January 20, 2010, from http://michaelhyatt .com/2009/12/why-vision-matters.html.

4. The Incrementalist (or What's the Small Idea?): An Interview with Joe Fox. *MIT Sloan Management Review*, 2008, *48*(4), p. 15.

5. Ibid, p. 20.

6. This classification system, with the acronym DEGEST, was developed by Northwestern University marketing professor Philip Kotler, and you can read more about it: Philip Kotler, *Marketing Management, 13th Edition*. New York: Prentice Hall, 2008. See also Edward Cornish, *Futuring: The Exploration of the Future*. Bethesda, MD: The World Future Society, 2005.

7. Warren Bennis, "Only the Optimists Survive." *BusinessWeek*, posted May 18, 2009; retrieved January 20, 2010, from http://www.businessweek.com/managing/content/may2009/ca20090518_917239.htm.

8. Norman Cousins, *Head First: The Biology of Hope and the Healing Power of the Human Spirit*. New York: E. P. Dutton, 1989, p. 83.

9. Martin E. P. Seligman, *Learned Optimism: How to Change Your Mind and Your Life*. New York: The Free Press, 1998.

TRUTH FIVE

1. Telephone interview with Jodi Taylor, then at the Center for Creative Leadership, Colorado Springs, Colorado, April 1998. See also V. I. Sessa and J. J. Taylor, *Executive Selection: Strategies for Success*. San Francisco: Jossey-Bass, 2000.

2. Daniel Goleman, *Emotional Intelligence: Why It Can Be More Than IQ* (10th Anniversary Edition). New York: Bantam Dell, 2006.

3. C. Fernández-Aráoz, "The Challenge of Hiring Senior Executives," in C. Cherniss and D. Goleman (eds.), *The Emotionally Intelligent Workplace: How to Select for, Measure, and Improve Emotional Intelligence in Individuals, Groups, and Organizations*. San Francisco:

Jossey-Bass, 2001, p. 189. Portions of the information were also gathered from personal correspondence and conversations (April 2010) with Claudio Fernández-Aráoz.

4. Morgan W. McCall and Michael M. Lombardo, *Off the Track: Why and How Successful Executives Get Derailed.* Greensboro, NC: Center for Creative Leadership, 1983.

5. Daniel Goleman, Richard E. Boyatzis, and Annie McKee, *Primal Leadership: Realizing the Power of Emotional Intelligence.* Boston: Harvard Business School Press, 2004, p. 5.

6. Ibid, pp. 19–31.

7. For more about meaning and other internal motivators, see Kenneth W. Thomas, *Intrinsic Motivation: What Really Drives Employee Engagement, Second Edition.* San Francisco: Berrett-Koehler, 2009.

8. James M. Kouzes and Barry Z. Posner, *A Leader's Legacy.* San Francisco: Jossey-Bass, 2006; in particular, see Chapter 13, "It's Not Just the Leader's Vision."

9. *As Good as It Gets.* Film directed by James L. Brooks, story and screenplay by Mark Andrus and James L. Brooks. Produced by James L. Brooks and Bridget Johnson. Production Companies, TriSTar Pictures and Gracie Films; distributed by Sony Pictures Entertainment, 1997.

10. John Hamm, "The Five Messages Leaders Must Manage." *Harvard Business Review*, May 2006, p. 7.

TRUTH SIX

1. Michael Segalla, "How Europeans Do Layoffs." Posted on the *Harvard Business Review* website June 9, 2009, http://blogs

.harvardbusiness.org/hbr/hbr-now/2009/06/how-europeans-do-layoffs.html. Accessed January 22, 2009. For access to the data on trust, see "Managing Talent in Troubled Times" at http://appli7.hec.fr/hrm/diversity/HBR_HEC_Executive_Survey1.htm. Retrieved January 22, 2010.

2. P. Shockley-Zalabak, S. Morreale, and M. Hackman, *Building the High Trust Organization*. San Francisco: Jossey-Bass, 2010.

3. D. Zand, "Trust and Managerial Problem Solving." *Administrative Science Quarterly*, 1972, *17*, pp. 230–239.

4. P. J. Sweeney, V. Thompson, and H. Blanton, "Trust and Influence in Combat: An Interdependence Model." *Journal of Applied Social Psychology*, 2009, *39*(1), pp. 235–264.

5. J. J. Gabarro, "The Development of Trust, Influence, and Expectations." In A. Athos and J. Gabarro (eds.), *Interpersonal Behavior: Communication and Understanding in Relationships* (pp. 290–303). Englewood Cliffs, NJ: Prentice Hall, 1978.

6. As quoted in Shockley-Zalabak, et al., *Building the High Trust Organization*. San Francisco: Jossey-Bass, 2010, p. 145.

7. "Customer Service Champs." *BusinessWeek*, March 2, 2009, pp. 32–33.

8. Roger Fisher and Scott Brown, *Getting Together*. Boston: Houghton Mifflin, 1988; James M. Kouzes and Barry Z. Posner, *Credibility*. San Francisco: Jossey-Bass, 2003.

9. As quoted in P. Shockley-Zalabak, et al., *Building the High Trust Organization*. San Francisco: Jossey-Bass, 2010, p. 79.

10. "A Little More Conversation: Employee Communications Approaches and Their Impact." A CHA report, Autumn 2005, p. 2. Accessed January 22, 2010, http://zookri.com/Portals/6/reports/A%20little%20more.pdf.

TRUTH SEVEN

1. John Gardner, speech, 1965. See http://www.pbs.org/ johngardner/chapters/4.html.

2. You can listen to the entire "The Last Lecture" on YouTube. It's well worth the seventy-six minutes of your time. See http://www.youtube.com/watch?v=ji5_MqicxSo.

3. Randy Pausch, *The Last Lecture: Achieving Your Childhood Dreams.* Video accessible at http://www.youtube.com/ watch?v=ji5_MqicxSo&feature=player_embedded. For more about Randy Pausch's story, see Randy Pausch with Jeffrey Zaslow, *The Last Lecture.* New York: Hyperion, 2008.

4. For more tips on how to be resilient in the face of stressful change, see Salvatore R. Maddi and Deborah M. Khoshaba, *Resilience at Work: How to Succeed No Matter What Life Throws at You.* New York: AMACOM, 2005.

5. B. Z. Posner, "Understanding the Learning Tactics of College Students and Their Relationship to Leadership," *Leadership & Organization Development Journal*, 2009, *30*(4), pp. 386–395; B. Z. Posner and J. W. Harder, "The Proactive Personality, Leadership, Gender and National Culture," paper presented at the Academy of Management (Western: Santa Fe), March 2002; and B. Z. Posner and L. M. Brown, "Exploring the Relationship Between Learning and Leadership," *Leadership & Organization Development Journal*, 2001, *22*(6), pp. 274–280.

6. Angela L. Duckworth, Christopher Peterson, Michael D. Matthews, and Dennis R. Kelly, "Personality Processes and

Individual Differences." *Journal of Personality and Social Psychology*, 2007, *92*(6), pp. 1087–1088.

7. Jonah Lehrer, "The Truth About Grit: Modern Science Builds Case for an Old-Fashioned Virtue—and Uncovers New Secrets to Success." *The Boston Globe*. Accessed August 2, 2009, on Boston.com from http://www.boston.com/bostonglobe/ideas/articles/2009/08/02/the_truth_about_grit?mode=PF.

8. Angela L. Duckworth, Christopher Peterson, Michael D. Matthews, and Dennis R. Kelly, "Personality Processes and Individual Differences." *Journal of Personality and Social Psychology*, 2007, *92*(6), p. 1096.

9. Ibid.

TRUTH EIGHT

1. From an interview with David Amram in Alex Zuckerman, *Wisdom*. New York: Abrams, 2008, p. 26.

2. Alan Deutschman, *Walk the Talk: The #1 Rule for Real Leaders*. New York: Portfolio, 2009, p. xii.

3. Tony Simons, "The High Cost of Lost Trust." *Harvard Business Review*, *80*(9), September 2002, p. 19. See also Tony Simons, *The Integrity Dividend*. San Francisco: Jossey-Bass, 2008.

4. D. K. McNeese-Smith, "Increasing Employee Productivity, Job Satisfaction, and Organizational Commitment." *Hospital & Health Services Administration*, 1996, *41*(2), pp. 160–175.

5. "Students Drive Principal to Roof." *San Jose Mercury News,* January 12, 2002, p. 3B.

6. Kirk Hanson, presentation for the Executive MBA Program, Leavey School of Business, Santa Clara University (Santa Clara, CA), 2008.

7. J. M. Kouzes and B. Z. Posner, *The Leadership Practices Inventory.* San Francisco: Pfeiffer, 2003. Available at http://as .leadershipchallenge.com/WileyCDA/Section/id-131060.html.

TRUTH NINE

1. Speech at 2009 Women of Distinction ceremony, June 4, 2009. A video of her speech can be found on YouTube at http://www.youtube.com/watch?v=8QMyECutpQo.

2. Barry Z. Posner, "A Longitudinal Study Examining Changes in Students' Leadership Behavior." *Journal of College Student Development*, 2009, *50*(5), pp. 551-563.

3. Barry Z. Posner and Lillas M. Brown, "Exploring the Relationship Between Learning and Leadership." *Leadership & Organization Development Journal*, 2001, *22*(6), pp. 274-280; and Barry Z. Posner, "Understanding the Learning Tactics of College Students and Their Relationship to Leadership." *Leadership & Organization Development Journal*, 2009, *30*(4), pp. 386-395.

4. To learn more about The Five Practices of Exemplary Leadership®, see James M. Kouzes and Barry Z. Posner, *The Leadership Challenge*, *4th Edition.* San Francisco, CA: Jossey-Bass, 2007.

5. Robert W. Eichinger, Michael M. Lombardo, and Dave Ulrich, *100 Things You Need to Know: Best Practices for Managers & HR.* Minneapolis, MN: Lominger, Ltd., 2004, p. 492.

6. Ibid, p. 495.

7. Thomas Friedman, *The World Is Flat.* New York: Farrar, Straus, and Giroux, 2006, p. 309.

8. Carol S. Dweck, *Mindset: The New Psychology of Success.* New York: Random House, 2006, p. 7.

9. Ibid, p. 6.

10. A. Bandura and R. E. Wood, "Effects of Perceived Controllability and Performance Standards on Self-Regulation of Complex Decision Making." *Journal of Personality and Social Psychology*, 1989, *56*, pp. 805–814.

11. See Dweck, *Mindset* (note #8), for a discussion of numerous research studies in all these and other domains.

12. Janet Rae-DuPree, "If You're Open to Growth, You Tend to Grow." *New York Times*, July 6, 2008. Accessed January 24, 2010, and retrievable from http://www.nytimes.com/2008/07/06/business/06unbox.html.

13. K. Anders Ericsson, "The Influence of Experience and Deliberate Practice on the Development of Superior Expert Performance." In K. Anders Ericsson, Neil Charness, Paul J. Feltovich, and Robert R. Hoffman (eds.), *The Cambridge Handbook of Expertise and Expert Performance.* New York: Cambridge University Press, 2006, p. 699.

14. See K. Anders Ericsson, 2006, p. 692. (See note #13.) Others have also written about this metric. See, for example, Geoff Colvin, *Talent Is Overrated: What Really Separates*

World-Class Performers from Everybody Else (New York: Portfolio, 2008); Daniel Coyle, *The Talent Code: Greatness Isn't Born. It's Grown. Here's How* (New York: Bantam Books, 2009); and Malcolm Gladwell, *Outliers: The Story of Success* (New York: Little Brown and Company, 2008).

15. K. Anders Ericsson, Michael J. Prietula, and Edward T. Cokely, "The Making of an Expert," *Harvard Business Review*, July–August 2007, reprint R0707J, p. 3.

16. Geoff Colvin, *Talent Is Overrated: What Really Separates World-Class Performers from Everybody Else*. New York: Portfolio, 2008, pp. 67–72.

17. Abraham Carmeli, Daphna Brueller, and Jane E. Dutton. "Learning Behaviours in the Workplace: The Role of High-Quality Interpersonal Relationships and Psychological Safety." *Systems Research and Behavioral Science Systems Research*, 2009, *26*, pp. 81–98.

18. Bonnie Hagemann and Judy Chartrand, "2009/2010 Trends in Executive Development: A Benchmark Report." Executive Development Associates, 2009, p. 15. Accessible at http://leadershipdevelopmenttrends.com.

19. K. Anders Ericsson, Michael J. Prietula, and Edward T. Cokely, "The Making of an Expert." *Harvard Business Review*, July–August 2007, reprint R0707J, p. 3.

TRUTH TEN

1. Parker J. Palmer, *Let Your Life Speak: Listening for the Voice of Vocation*. San Francisco: Jossey-Bass, 2000, p. 76.

2. J. M. Kouzes and B. Z. Posner, "Ethical Leaders: An Essay About Being in Love." *Journal of Business Ethics*, 1992, *11*, pp. 479–484.

3. R. J. Ferris, "How Organizational Love Can Improve Leadership." *Organizational Dynamics*, 1988, *16*(4), pp. 41–51.

4. R. K. Greenleaf, *Servant Leadership*. New York: Paulist Press, 2002.

5. "My Bad Boss." *San Jose Mercury News*, November 2, 2008, p. 3E, www.mercurynews.com.

6. W. A. Wines and J. B. Hamilton III, "On Changing Organizational Cultures by Injecting New Ideologies: The Power of Stories." *Journal of Business Ethics*, 2009, *89*, pp. 433–447.

7. J. F. McCarthy, "Short Stories at Work." *Group & Organization Management*, 2008, *33*(2), pp. 163–193.

8. Beth Kurylo, "Storytelling Boosts Child Confidence, Say Emory Researchers." Available at http://www.communitelligence.com/npps/story.cfm?nppage=95. Posted October 10, 2005; retrieved January 24, 2010.

9. BMO+Harris@Work (internal company publication), August/September 2006, p. 9.

10. Stephen J. Dubner and Steven D. Levitt, "A Star Is Made." *New York Times*, May 7, 2006. Available at http://www.nytimes.com/2006/05/07/magazine/07wwln_freak.html?_r=1&ei=5070&en=c0acc9bb46cdeef4&ex=1162270800&pagewanted=print. Posted May 7, 2006; retrieved December 30, 2009.

11. Barbara L. Fredrickson, *Positivity: Groundbreaking Research Reveals How to Embrace the Hidden Strengths of Positive Emotions, Overcome Negativity, and Thrive.* New York: Crown Publishers, 2009, p. 21.

12. Ibid, pp. 60–65.

13. Marcial Losada and Emily Heaphy, "The Role of Positivity and Connectivity in the Performance of Business Teams: A Nonlinear Dynamics Model." *American Behavioral Scientist*, 2004, 47(6), pp. 740–765.

14. Ibid, p. 747.

15. Barbara L. Fredrickson and Marcial F. Losada, "Positive Affect and the Complex Dynamics of Human Flourishing." *American Psychologist*, 2005, *60*(7), pp. 678–686.

EPILOGUE

1. For another important perspective on "saying yes," see Patricia Ryan Madson, *Improv Wisdom: Don't Prepare, Just Show Up*. New York: Bell Tower, 2005.

2. For a complete biography of Ivana Sendecka, see http://ivanasendecka.com.

3. Ron A. Carucci, *Leadership Divided: What Emerging Leaders Need and What You Might Be Missing*. San Francisco: Jossey-Bass, 2006.

4. Ivana's initial team consisted of Ron Carucci and Josh Epperson from Passages Consulting in Seattle, Washington; Jon DeWaal of DeWaal Painting Company in Seattle, Washington; and Veronika Kopcik of Research Bridge in Waterloo, Ontario, Canada.

5. You can hear Ivana tell her story in her own words by viewing her video blogpost at http://ivanasendecka.com/2010/02/08/bodyguard-for-your-dreams. Accessed February 14, 2010.

6. President Michael Hogan, University of Connecticut, commencement address, May 10, 2009; available online at http://www.commencement.uconn.edu/history/audio/; accessed February 18, 2010.

INDEX